Three Links of Chain

Three Links of Chain

a novel

Dennis Maley

Jublio
Oklahoma City, OK

Jublio
Oklahoma City, OK
www.jubliobooks.com

Editor: Kristin Thiel
Cover Artist: S. A. Hunt
Book Designer: Jennifer Omner
Set in Rockwell and Adobe Caslon Pro

Publisher's Cataloging-in-Publication Data

Maley, Dennis.
   Three links of chain / Dennis Maley.
      pages cm
   ISBN: 978-0-9861158-0-6 (pbk.)
   ISBN: 978-0-9861158-1-3 (e-book)
   1. Slavery—Fiction. 2. Underground Railroad—Fiction.
3. Self-reliance—Fiction. 4. Kansas—Fiction.   I. Title.
PZ7.M2928 Th 2015
[Fic]—dc23

2015901540

Mary wore three links of chain,
On every link was freedom's name

1

— — —

"Georgie Porgie, puddin' and pie, kissed the girls and made them cry!"

"Knock it off!" Blanche scolded. "Did you come here to sell papers or just sport around?"

It seemed like every day Blanche had to put up with the same kind of horseplay from the white paperboys that he supervised. One mocked the other, and the next thing he knew, they were whacking one another with their canvas bags.

"Hey! He's hitting me back!"

Blanche was a stocky young slave who was serious about his job and was proud of having learned to read. It was illegal for slaves to know how to read, but he knew that literate people had power—his mother told him so—and together they found a way for him to learn. He had accomplished his goal against the odds. Maybe sometimes his paperboys thought he was sniffy, acting arrogant or important, because he never allowed himself any time for this kind of foolishness, skylarking with friends, or tormenting himself with girls. He refused to call himself by the disgusting word, the epithet, that slaves and owners all used. If Blanche referred to his race, he called himself a Negro. He had pride.

"There's folks here trying to use this sidewalk," he said to the paperboys, who paid him no mind.

Blanche was fourteen. A colorful tie held the collar of his long-sleeved white shirt closed around his neck. He wore elbow-length black fabric covers to protect the forearms and cuffs of his shirt from ink stains. Right now he needed to get his rowdy paperboys off their duffs. Or rather, he thought as he watched them skip between passersby, he didn't need to get them off their rear ends—he needed to get them organized and on task. The paper didn't sell itself, and several bundles of papers blocked his way to the bulletin board that was on the storefront of his master's print shop. He needed a little elbow-room so he could tack up a flyer.

Blanche's withering glare was what it took. He could have them fired on a moment's notice. Each boy grabbed his bundle of papers, and the pile melted away.

As he tacked the flyer up, he found himself proof-reading it once again out of force of habit.

RUNAWAY! $500 Reward! Runaway from the subscriber, living in Cass County, on the 4th of June, a Negro Man, named Jim aged about 25 years. Jim is dish-faced; has sore eyes and bad teeth; is of a light black or brown color; speaks quick; is about 5 feet 7 inches high; has a very small foot, wears perhaps a No. 6 shoe, and has heavy tacks in the heels; had on when last seen, blue cotton pants, white shirt, white fulled coat and new custom-made boots. Jim is doubtless aiming for Kansas Territory and on to Nebraska City, Nebraska Territory. A reward of $500 will be given if taken outside of the State, or $250 if taken in the State, outside of Cass County. C. D. Williams, Hadsell P. O., Cass County, Missouri. Westport, Missouri, March 2 1855.

It wasn't the first runaway flyer Blanche had printed, and it wasn't likely to be the last. Blanche considered taking down some of the aged and tattered business notices and yellowed calling cards that littered the bulletin board. *Next time,* he thought. He was in a little bit of a hurry. He needed to pee.

Blanche was born in Virginia. His father was a white planter and his mother was a Negro house slave. His father claimed him as his property but not as his son. Even though he was half white, his father, a son of the South, considered him all black.

Blanche figured out his parentage by eavesdropping on what the house slaves gossiped about, crouched behind the handrail in a central atrium of the planter's great house where the slaves were allowed to listen to Sunday sermons. The second floor had a grand gallery under a dome that reflected and magnified the voices from below. He also listened in on the tutor's lessons given to the planter's legitimate son, as he was considered, because his mother was white and married to his father. In that way, Blanche also learned to read and write and do his sums. Blanche was careful that no one but his mother knew. The law punished slaves if they learned to read.

When Blanche was just ten years old, that planter found himself in a countrywide financial panic. The price of cotton had dropped as if it had fallen off the table. To hedge his losses, his father put him and his mother on the auction block. One day Blanche had been helping his mother with laundry, and the next he and his mother and several other slaves were herded into a wagon and taken to town. No one was permitted to leave with valuables, not even a stitch of extra clothes beyond those on his back. Blanche was confused. Dread set in when he saw terror in his mother's face, her features twisted as if in agony. Men, women, and children—every eye filled with tears. The women pleaded with their master for mercy. "Pray, Marse, sell us as a family." The master tried to speak but choked on his words. Then he turned away.

Blanche's mother dried her eyes and pulled Blanche to her side. She whispered to him with urgency. "Now you learn this and learn it real good. If a man asks you, 'Have you been on the railroad,' you must tell him, 'I have been a short distance.' Let me hear you say it."

"I have been a short distance."

"Then he's going to ask, 'Where did you start from? And you say, 'The depot.'"

"The depot."

"Then he says, 'Where did you stop?' and you say, 'At a place called safety.'"

His body shook as it never had. Hauled away to be sold and all his mother could think about was some mad nursery rhyme. He told himself that the tears he shed were for his mother's insanity, but it was the fear of what lay ahead, fear of the unknown that gripped him. He clung to his mother, buried his face in her apron. It smelled of cornbread; it smelled of home. This country house was his only world, where all his friends—including even the planter's white son— lived. It was his home and he knew he would never see it again. Now his only hope was that he and his mother would be sold as a pair. If they weren't, she would have no one to protect her, and he would have no one to cling to when thunder rattled the sky. Ignoring their pleas, the agents who conducted the auction ripped them apart. His mother cried out in vain, "Pray sell us together. My son."

Blanche was driven ahead of the other men and into a corral. Out of the shouts of the women behind him, he heard only his mother's anguished screams. He never saw her again. He did not know if she was sold or not and never had any way to find out. He was afraid of the slavemasters, but more than that, it was grief that buckled his knees. His mother might as well be dead to him, but he prayed for her safety.

The agents described Blanche as "prime stock." The bidders laughed at the sight of the bawling boy with snot running down his face.

A carpenter named Tullis bid $200 for Blanche. The auctioneer shouted, "Sold to the man in the coveralls!" and slammed a gavel on his makeshift table. Blanche wiped the mucus from his face and the tears from his eyes. He looked his new owner over head to toe. *At least he's not a farmer,* Blanche told himself. The farmers who owned slaves treated their field hands like animals. He didn't think he could bear that life.

They headed west. As he and his new master crossed the wide Mississippi River at Saint Louis, Blanche swore by his soul that he wouldn't cry himself to sleep anymore. He kept his promise as their journey took them over the high ground on the south side of the Missouri River, first to Sedalia, Missouri, and then on to the last outpost on the westward roads, Westport, Missouri.

Westport was a brawling nowhere, the last stop on the road to somewhere else. The road continued, but it led only out into a prairie that was so broad it took weeks to cross. The part that ran through town was filled with cattle drovers, gamblers, land speculators, settlers in covered wagons headed west, and Mexicans from Santa Fe. The Americans called them "Spaniards." If Blanche had stood at the town's western border and thrown a stone with not much effort at all, it would have landed in Kansas Territory.

He tried desperately to do as his master demanded of him, out of fear of getting put back on the auction block, or worse. Still, Blanche had difficulty earning his keep. They worked in the trades, building houses that clustered around the town. Tullis said his young slave "wasn't much for making up window sashes." He couldn't keep up. But Blanche was lucky—with barely a pause, Tullis put him out to work for Henry, a printer who catered to the mercantile vultures of Westport. Not a bad deal for Tullis, who collected Blanche's wages. Tullis had to pay for Blanche's food, shelter, and clothing, and the only other hitch was collecting his money from Henry, who had a bad habit of making himself scarce at the end of the month, Tullis's payday.

Not many slaves lived near Westport, but most of those who did, like Blanche, worked for wages. Their masters lived off of the money their labor earned. Boarding houses and the trades offered steady employment. Many slaves were hired out to cut timber or build railroad tracks. The rest worked as farm laborers, tending cattle and hogs and raising vegetables for the market: corn, potatoes, tomatoes, beans, and squash. Big row crops like cotton and tobacco failed to thrive in the climate, so Missouri didn't have plantations like those Blanche knew from growing up in Virginia.

Henry saw an advantage when he realized that Blanche could read. The slave boy was so quick to pick up the skills a printer needed that he had to be literate. Blanche was delighted to work for Henry.

He had a chance to learn a trade that was an almost sacred calling.

Henry was a clever manipulator and usually got his way. He just had to convince Tullis that selling Blanche was in Tullis's best interest.

"Land sakes, Tullis, don't you ever feed that kid? He'd eat a body out of house and home."

Tullis didn't care about that—a slave could survive on bread and beans—but he rubbed his chin and thought about all the days he'd wasted chasing Henry for money. "You got an offer?"

"It'll take you a year to make what I'll give you even if you didn't feed him."

Blanche's ownership changed hands again, this time for $150, cash on the barrelhead. Tullis didn't trust Henry and the only way he would sell is if he got all of his cash, up front.

"I'm glad to be shed of him and Henry too," Tullis said to himself.

Blanche, his first flyer posted and loaded down with a canvas bag full of more freshly printed papers, exited the brawling roadway by way of an alleyway between the buildings. A public outhouse occupied the space at the end of several worn footpaths behind the stores. To his left, he spotted his master, Henry, on a beeline to the backhouse. At the same moment, a planter named Williams came down a third path. He had an urgent look on his face and was trucking toward the same destination. Blanche quickly did the sums. Three bodies plus a two-hole privy did not equal anything in his favor. The white men ratcheted up their speed. Together, Henry and Williams elbowed their way through the swinging door of the outhouse, and Blanche was left outside to wait for a turn.

He pulled open the door and handed a paper to Williams. "Here's one of your flyers, Marse Williams." Williams and Henry both sat on a flat shelf with their drawers around their ankles. Williams grabbed the handbill and slammed the door shut.

Blanche stood on one foot. Then the other. He was accustomed to waiting in line, but his need was growing urgent, and all he could do was listen in. Master Henry was yammering on about "the peculiar institution of slavery." As ever.

A nest of paper wasps buzzed under the eaves of the outhouse, and Blanche considered poking it with a stick. He'd done just that before, amused to see white men scramble out of the privy, but he didn't want angry wasps bothering him when it was his turn.

"You misspelled *subscriber,*" Williams's voice whined.

"No, I didn't," Blanche whispered.

"And land sakes, boy, you put a *B* in *doubtless*."

"That's the way…" Blanche bit his tongue. He wanted to correct Williams's error, but knew he was in for a whipping if Williams discovered he could read. "That's the way Marse Henry spells it. I just copies."

"You trying to…*read*? You got jittery ideas? Gonna run off a fugitive like my boy Jim?"

"Run off? Not me. I got it good here."

"Lead a big revolt, maybe?"

"Shoot, Marse Williams. The best-looking Negro boy around these here parts?" Blanche knew from experience that it was best to play dumb around the slave owners. "I got no more use for an ignorant bunch of field hands than you do. And no, suh, I ain't leading no one, nowhere, no how. Shoot."

Henry had his own way of dealing with the customers of the print shop. "Take the *B* out, Blanche," he said. "We'll run another couple hundred, Williams. Only cost you four bits."

"Whatever you say, Marse Henry," Blanche agreed, then said impatiently, "but I need to use it. Could you hurry?"

But Williams wasn't ready to give up. "Folks around here are getting tired of you and your shakedowns, Henry."

"Noticed that white ribbon in your lapel, Mr. Williams," Henry said. "You headed out to Kansas next week?"

Henry's dodge worked. Williams forgot the flyers. "I doubt it," Williams said. "You?"

"I need to sell a slave first. Supposed to be a buyer in from Saint Louis."

Blanche leaned his forehead against the rough siding of the outhouse. He didn't know how much longer he could hold it.

"What ya got?" Williams asked.

"A big buck field hand. Sound as a dollar." A sick feeling hit Blanche in the pit of his stomach. Henry had to be talking about selling a slave named Reuben. He was only a field hand, old enough to be his father, but he was kind to Blanche, a big brother in a way, and always helped him stay out of trouble.

"What you asking?"

"Twelve hundred."

"Twelve hundred!" Williams whistled.

Blanche's mind was spinning. What was bad news for Reuben might be good news for Blanche. If Henry was primed to sell, maybe he would entertain an offer from Blanche.

"You wearing a ribbon but not going to vote?" Henry asked.

"Nah. I don't think I want to stay drunk for three days. Seems like that's what an election turns into. Can't afford it, not with my Jim running off and all."

Henry grew more serious. "Missouri men got as much right to vote in Kansas as them free state cowards. Voting the rooster ain't a right; it's a sacred duty."

Blanche's feet danced now. Even as Williams exited the outhouse, his broad body blocked the entrance. Blanche couldn't squeeze past.

"Last election people was so snot-slinging drunk that half of them didn't even take a ballot."

"Ain't gonna let that happen again. I printed up six thousand. Used a pretty, kinda sky-blue paper stock."

"You think that's enough?"

The question insulted Henry. "There's only three thousand people fool enough to live out there. Tumbleweeds and Indians. Throw out the women and kids, and there ain't enough Whigs in Kansas Territory to give a cat a good cussing. Six thousand ballots is plenty."

Blanche redirected his thoughts from his bladder to Henry's words. Slaves couldn't vote, but neither could white women or Indians. One political party, the Whigs, stood against slavery's expansion into the territories, the places like Kansas Territory that would someday become states. If the country admitted free states, then that would mean Congress would have more representatives and senators who wanted slavery abolished. Since that would dilute the power of the slave states, like Missouri, Henry and Williams hated Whigs.

"Fools. Cowards. Jayhawkers. You fix the spelling, boy, and I'll be back later for the rest." Williams mumbled to himself as hoisted his drawers, looped galluses over his shoulders, and waddled away from the outhouse with his flyers.

Blanche scrambled into the outhouse and relieved himself alongside the seated Henry. "Marse Henry, I've been thinking maybe I could just maybe buy myself out from under you. Since you're in a trading mood." As a slave, Blanche didn't have much in the way of material possessions, but he had some money hidden away, money earned working odd jobs at night.

"Eh, I don't think so, Blanche."

"I'd pay you what I'm worth."

"You'll get your freepapers when I put on the wooden overcoat." Blanche could see from the way Henry joked about his coffin, about his own mortality, that he didn't take the offer seriously. "It's in my will."

"Marse Henry, I want to be a freeman now. I'll pay more than what I'm worth."

"I'll ponder on it," Henry said.

Blanche believed Henry actually liked him. But from working alongside his master, Blanche knew that as far as Henry was concerned, business was business. Henry was never unfairly mean to him and had taught him a lot—but Henry never made a commitment he didn't have to make.

Henry picked the softest looking corncob from a bucket in the corner and used it to scrape his backside before tugging up his trousers. As he left the outhouse, he told his slave, "I'll ponder on it, but I don't think so."

Blanche regretted that he had wasted the chance to angry up that nest of paper wasps that buzzed under the eaves of the outhouse.

2

— — —

On the north side of Westport's one rutted roadway, a pro-slavery political rally gathered steam. With the election looming, these gatherings happened every week.

Blanche couldn't understand why the Missourians wasted so much effort mustering up for slavery or why Henry put so many pro-slavery articles in the newspaper. As far as he could see, it was as if they were shouting about wanting more blue skies. The white folks were masters, and the black folks were slaves. That was the way things had always been and the way things were always going to be. All the meetings and flag waving in the world wouldn't change that a lick.

So as he headed to the print shop, Blanche's attention was drawn not to the rally but to raucous laughter coming from above the road. Looking out over the fray, a half dozen men and women whooped it up on the balcony of a saloon that called itself the Cyprian Sisterhood. In polite company, Henry called the working girls from the saloon *painted ladies*, *soiled doves*, or *sporting women*. His master and his friends used names that were much crueler than that when they joked about them in private. Their job was to coax cash out of the pockets of their coarse and lonely customers with a wink, a saucy story, a laugh, a dance. If they did their jobs well, the saloon owners sold more whiskey. The working girls sold their kisses—and more—to the gamblers, speculators, and cattle drovers and hoped to find a good husband to help free them from their own kind of slavery.

In the middle of the company on the balcony was a lean fellow, square jawed, with dark, relentless, burning eyes. He wore tall riding boots and a military tunic. Yet he was half out of uniform—he wore no trousers, only long-handled underwear.

Blanche had never before seen the newcomer, but he was sure that he was Colonel Jim Lane. Henry's columns this last week had been full of puffed-up stories about the man's life history and his visit to Westport. He had enlisted in the Mexican War as a private, quickly risen through the ranks to colonel, and had first earned notice for having rallied a scattered regiment to turn and defeat the enemy. His political affiliation was Democrat, but he was a warrior first and foremost. Henry's writings led Blanche to expect Lane to be some Scots-Irish chieftain mounted on a fire-breathing horse.

Blanche couldn't take his eyes off of Jim Lane, and neither could the people in his company. He was a clean-shaven man of forty, and at well over six feet, he was uncommonly tall, with a long face under a high forehead, and gangling arms with bony fingers. He had an elegant, flamboyant, confident swagger, a quick grin, and a quicker scowl. The paperboys all knew his name and repeated what they had heard from their fathers, that Colonel Lane was certain to get an important command if another war broke out. They made a pact to join his regiment when they were old enough. They swore to fight for any fiery cause if Lane was their leader.

"The pen is mightier than the sword," Blanche told the boys, repeating something he'd heard Henry say a thousand times over. Colonel Lane and every boozy layabout in Westport could rally to preserve slavery until the cows came home as far as Blanche was concerned. Nothing needed to change as long as he had a chance to purchase his freedom.

Today, Colonel Lane was buttering up a big shot from Washington City, the nation's capital, Senator David Atchison.

While Blanche gathered up his hammer and tacks

and stuffed a stack of flyers into his canvas bag, he eavesdropped on the men on the balcony. He didn't have to strain to hear, because the boozy Atchison brayed like a donkey. Lane's voice carried over the noise as well.

"In 1849, President James Polk's term ended at noon on Sunday, and out of reverence for the Sabbath, Zachary Taylor refused to take the oath of office until Monday. Myself, as president pro tempore of the Senate, stood third in line. So, for that one day, I was president."

"What did you do?" asked Lane.

"I went to bed. We had had two or three all-night sessions, finishing up the work, so I went to bed and slept. That was the honest-est administration this country ever had."

Lane laughed way too hard, and Blanche suspected he'd heard the story a hundred times before. A broad smile lit up Atchison's face.

"Quieten down now—let's see what that gasbag Stringfellow has on his feeble mind," Lane told his fellow revelers. The noise from the balcony died down. Even big shots did Colonel Lane's bidding.

"Mark every scoundrel that has the least taint of abolitionism," the man who must have been String-fellow was shouting to the crowd. "Exterminate him. Don't give a quarter to the rascals. Mark them in this street, on this day, crush them out!" Cheers interrupted Stringfellow's speech. "The law must be disregarded. Your lives and property are in danger. Enter every election in Kansas Territory! To hell with Reeder and his vile Yankees. Vote at the point of the Bowie knife and revolver. Our cause demands it. Let there be no appeal! What right has Governor Reeder to rule Missourians in Kansas? His proclamations are worthless. His oath means nothing. I tell you today, this is what we want. Slavery established! From the Atlantic to the Pacific! Everywhere!"

Blanche thought Stringfellow's last *everywhere* sounded like a death rattle. It fell away into a growl and disappeared into a drunken shout of approval from the rough-scuff street crowd of drunks.

The New York Times called Westport's rabble of pro-slavery rowdies "border ruffians." The abolition folks in town and visitors from Iowa called them "Missouri pukes." Blanche particularly liked that one. He laughed up his sleeve when white people had ugly things to say about one another.

Blanche heard them both—Missouri puke and border ruffian—on the sidewalk outside the print shop. The pro-slavery bunch embraced both nicknames. They liked to think of themselves as wings of political parties, but they were nothing more than drinking clubs, plain and simple.

Stringfellow slammed a fist into his hand to signal the crowd that he had nothing more to say. "Buy him a drink," Colonel Lane shouted. The Colonel deftly brushed off a whiskey offered to him by the scantily clad painted lady who fondled his medals. He didn't drink alcohol himself, but he never shunned a woman who wanted to press herself into his side and whisper into his ear with a giggle.

Lane's eyes sought out his wife, Mary, who sat below in a buggy. Mary's brittle, unsmiling face glowered into a book, her eyes undeviating, as if the rampage of the border ruffians was taking place a hundred miles away, as if her husband's scandalous behavior on the balcony above was taking place in Washington City, instead of Westport.

"So, what about my lots?" Atchison's voice bellowed over the cheers of the swarm that still rallied Stringfellow's speech. "Want to buy them?"

The question amused Colonel Lane. "You're mighty eager, Senator Atchison. What's wrong with your land? It underwater?"

"You're awful suspicious. Last chance."

"Find another sucker."

"We need settlers like you and your missus."

Colonel Lane shook his head. "I got work to do"—jabbing a long finger toward Kansas Territory in the west—"out in Douglas County." Lane had been promised political patronage by Senator Douglas, but he had made a more important promise to himself. He would never be satisfied until the last anti-slavery voter in Kansas was run out of the Territory. He would be rich, but money meant little. He wanted power.

Samuel Jones tossed a moneybag to Lane. "I just sold a slave, and I reckon this is my share toward cleaning every stinking Yankee coward plumb out of Kansas Territory." Jones was tall and thin with a cadaverous complexion. His sullen eyes avoided contact. He was one of Atchison's toadies. The thirty-or-so, cigar-chomping, profane postmaster of Westport was a loyal party man who would have licked Atchison's boots if he'd been asked. Still, his postmaster appointment had cost him a bundle.

Colonel Lane was disappointed; he expected to be treated to a little more glad-handing from the party regulars. "Chalk this up to seed money, Jones," said Lane, stuffing the purse in his breast pocket. "After the election, money's gonna flow your way like that old river."

A gunshot rang out, and the rowdy crowd of thugs yelled itself to life again. From the far end of the muddy street, two saloon girls raced toward a makeshift finish line that stretched across the way in the front of the saloon. One runner was white, one black.

They both wore nothing but their undergarments, and they slipped and slid in the ankle-deep mire through a course bordered by the cheering ruffians.

"Lay you twenty, Jones," Lane said.

"Gimme odds."

"Twenty eighteen."

"Call twenty fifteen."

"You're on."

"I'll take the blackie," said Jones.

Lane nodded. "You're on." Colonel Lane looked down at his wife and gave her a high and mighty smile. Her face drew up as tight as a drumhead. Tears welled in her eyes.

Lane looked away to see the black girl pull ahead, and as she did, a spectator shot his leg out across the raceway. Her shin smacked flush into the hurdle that she hadn't seen. Her feet flew out behind, and upended, she fell, sprawling face-first into the mud. Even though she was blinded by the sticky sludge, she managed somehow to right herself, stood, and swung her fist in a wild roundhouse punch.

Her forearm caught the running white woman under the chin, and both women fell into the muck. Quicker than Lane could have said "get after it," the black woman climbed onto the back of the white gal and, shrieking like a banshee, sunk her teeth deep into her shoulder.

The ruffians broke ranks and encircled the fighting women. The footrace had blossomed into a wrestling match. The combatants exchanged ferocious punches, and the crowd pressed to rally either girl if she showed any sign of quitting. The engagement soon digressed to slapping and hair pulling.

The white men in Westport could not imagine that life could be more grand.

3

— — —

"When I put on the wooden overcoat." Every time Blanche had ever asked about buying his freedom, that's what Henry's answer had been. Blanche had no intention of waiting for Henry to die, of waiting to see his dead old bones buried deep in the ground in a wooden casket. Henry was a skinny little squirt and looked to be as healthy as a horse.

Blanche had been able to learn about the way things worked in the white man's world from newspapers and magazines left by guests at the boarding house. He hid them in his waistband and carried them home. *The New York Times* published a steady stream of abolition talk and, owing to the running conflicts along the border between slave and free states, it called the territory to the west "Bleeding Kansas." Another publication, *Frank Leslie's Illustrated Newspaper,* took up the name too, and filled its pages with woodcut illustrations of burning barns and churches. Tensions ran high in the ramp-up to the Kansas Territorial election.

He was eager to get his emancipation. Blanche always believed that someday he'd be free but never thought the abolition talk was anything more than Yankees flapping their jaws. He never doubted that he would be emancipated. So, now that Blanche had some cash saved, he reckoned that the day was just around the corner when he would be able to buy his freedom, and once he was free, his ability to read and run a press would open up doors for him everywhere. With a trade such as that, as well as a dream and some guts, no one in the world could hold him back. White folks even had a law to make sure a printer could write anything he wanted, no matter how outrageous, and put it down on paper for other white folks to read. If someone was ever to build an altar to freedom, it would have a printing press on it.

The printers were financial big shots. He'd been around white men and commerce enough to see it himself. They spent every waking hour trying to make a dollar. Henry never rested on his laurels; he did more than run a press. Henry made more money trading city lots than he did printing the paper, because if something went up for sale, the man at the print shop was the first to know. *The whites may be devils*, Blanche thought, *but they have what the Indians and the slaves don't have. They have the gumption to turn their dreams into reality.* Blanche didn't rest on his laurels either—he worked two jobs. One helping Henry at the print shop and the other serving food at the boarding house.

Yankees. No better than field hands, Blanche thought. *Abolition talk is crazy talk.* It was fine for the field hands to talk and sing and preach about freedom, but he was certain the day would never come when the owners would free all the slaves. It seemed to him that regardless of what they printed in *The New York Times*, owning slaves was a way of life for all white people—at least, all the white people he'd met; that was true in Virginia, Missouri, and probably New York City and everywhere else in the world. *The field hands can sing and talk about freedom all they want. Listening to them is just like listening to tall tales about the talking animals always trying to trick one another. Something to talk about. Just nonsense and false hope,* Blanche thought.

They are so ignorant. Even if they were freed tomorrow, what would they do? They have no plan! They'd end up homeless and penniless. Do they think the Indians got it better, starving and freezing all winter? When I'm free, I'll walk where I want to walk and say good morning to the folks I want to say good morning to and tip the brim of my hat with a silver handled cane.

Because I got a trade, and I got gumption. I might get so rich, I'll need to buy a slave for myself. And if I want to learn things, then all I got to do is get me a book and read up on it. Like why does the sun rise in the east in the morning and set in the west in the evening? Why is the sky blue and the grass green? Where do the birds go in the winter?

Inside the print shop, Henry stood by a tall cabinet full of shallow drawers. Each drawer was sectioned into little boxes, and each section held lead slugs with the mirror image of just one letter of the alphabet formed on one end. Each drawer held the full alphabet, just in different sizes, and every drawer was divided in exactly the same pattern. The typesetter knew if he picked a slug from the biggest box that he'd pull out an *e*. The smallest sections held *z* and *q*. Since each letter had a specific place in the drawer, a trained printer could set type blindfolded. Still, Henry wasn't as quick as he had been. He was starting to struggle.

The slugs in the lower drawers were small, but in the upper drawers, they were downright tiny. "My arms are too short to see these real good," Henry told Blanche, and ever more frequently he relied on his slave to set the smaller types. It was a tedious process, but Blanche was gaining speed. Soon he would be as fast as his master.

Henry was working out of a lower drawer. One by one, he selected slugs from the tray and clamped them into a metal box that was just as long and wide as a newspaper column. This was setting the type, according to Henry. The box would later pack into a flat metal tray filled with other boxes of set type. When all was to Henry's liking, he'd fasten the assembly into his printing press, give the monster a good inking, and "roll out the dough," as he liked to say. Henry was a small man, with long, slender hands, so in addition to setting the smallest type, all the heavy work—cranking the press and keeping the paper fed—fell to Blanche.

Today's editorial was a scathing indictment of an East Coast writer, a black abolitionist named Frederick Douglass. A few weeks earlier, Henry's editorial had ripped apart Harriet Beecher Stowe, the author of a novel that no one in Westport was reading anyway, *Uncle Tom's Cabin*. Henry's attacks on abolitionists were always fierce and personal. He'd never read a word Douglass had written, he boasted to Blanche, but he didn't hesitate to argue that a freeman could never have written that well. *I wouldn't read it,* Blanche thought, *even if I had the chance. It's probably nothing but a bunch of ideas. I will have time for ideas later, once I've saved up enough to buy myself. Big ideas can wait.*

Blanche turned the heavy flywheel of the press. He needed to finish the Williams job before moving on to crank out the newspaper. He noticed Henry eyeballing him, so he continued the conversation that Henry had broken off in the outhouse. "About what I was saying. Me buying my freedom…I think I can scrape together a few dollars. And then give you something every month until I get the debt paid off."

"We'll see," droned Henry. "We'll see. We'll see."

The front door of the shop opened and sounded a bell that hung from a loopy spring over the entry. Blanche recognized the customer as one of the sporting men he served at the boarding house. The gambler puffed on a long black cigar and wore a hat with a wide brim and a colorful silk waistcoat.

"Too late to place an ad?" He had to yell over the noise of the press.

"What you got?" Henry shot back.

"Needing to sell a couple of lots." As the gambler spoke, he handed Henry a slip of paper with his ad copy written on it. "I'm starting to think that maybe that faro dealer at the Sisterhood is a crook."

"Not on your life. He goes to my church. Why, he's the last man…The ad costs two bits," said Henry, taking the gambler's money. "But you're too late for today's paper. It'll run tomorrow."

The jingling doorbell drowned out the grumbling of the customer as he left the shop.

"When you said, 'We'll see,'" Blanche said over the noisy flywheel, "when were you thinking that we'll see?"

"Listen, I'm done talking about that. What I do want to talk about is if Williams had half a brain, he would have realized right there in the backhouse that you can read. I'll only get a fine. They'll whip you within an inch of your life."

"Yessir, Marse Henry." It was true. Blanche had to be more careful about letting white people know he could read. He knew lots of things that he kept his mouth shut about. *If that gambler had half a brain, he'd know the faro dealer was a crook, and he'd know Henry was going to try to cheat him on his lots.*

"Marse Henry, you mind if I overwork a couple of hours at the boarding house? Sure could use the money."

"All work and no play."

"I need admission money. There's gonna be a dance."

"Why didn't you say so? Nothing I like seeing any better than a bunch of slaves fiddling and dancing. You stay here in town if a bed is offered. No sense walking home."

"It's just a quarter mile, Marse Henry."

"On second thought, write yourself out a pass. You'll need it if the patrollers are out."

"Yessir, Marse Henry."

Henry removed his black apron and his black sleeve protectors. "I'm going to see a couple of lots that might be coming up for sale."

As Henry exited the print shop, a regular customer entered. "Just under the wire, Mr. Bensabat," he said.

"Nice weather for an election, Mr. Henry."

As Henry closed the door, Blanche smiled. He was always happy to see Bensabat, the only white man he counted as a friend. If Blanche spoke proper English to him or looked him in the eye, the merchant never fumed with anger like the other whites. He said once that his people had been slaves, but Blanche thought perhaps he was making that story up. He didn't have that scared-rabbit look of a man who had felt the whip. "We're putting the paper to bed here in a few minutes, Marse Bensabat."

"Not too late for one more ad?" Bensabat handed a slip of paper to Blanche that contained his store's ad copy. Blanche wrote out a receipt.

Bensabat advertised daily. Henry's big ledger book listed him under the letter *I*. Izzy's Cut-Price Dry Goods, Isadore Bensabat, Proprietor. The ledger page didn't disclose the epithet that Henry called him behind his back: "the damn Jew." If white people wanted to hate one another, it was no skin off of Blanche's nose.

"I don't need a receipt," the customer said. "Not from you anyway. Now, Henry—I wouldn't trust him as far as I can throw him."

"I get the papers to prove I'm not cheating him. I can't have him thinking I'm stealing. You still got my money in safe keeping?"

Bensabat turned to look over his shoulder before answering. "In my strongbox. Hundred eighty on the nose."

"A hundred and eighty dollars. Make a pretty good down payment."

"You earned every penny."

Blanche returned to the press. "I saved fifty dollars last year."

"A white pressman would cost Henry thirty a month."

"I'll buy my freepapers. You hide and watch."

Bensabat looked at a copy of Williams's flyer on the counter. "Maybe those runaways aren't so ignorant."

"Nothing but an ignorant field hand," said Blanche, over the clatter of the press. "Strong back. Weak mind."

"Listen to you," Bensabat scolded. "You'd do the same if they sold off your wife and kids."

Bensabat's ribbing had begun to get under Blanche's skin. "He's not the first to get sold off. And I worked my way into this print shop so I don't have to get treated like a field hand. Did it all on my own. Marse Henry treats me real good. Gives me plenty of good food. He lets me keep my wages when I overwork. Not everyone got a good master like that."

"That's not so unusual…"

"Maybe not, but he don't whip me and don't let anyone else whip me either."

"You even learned to read and write."

"You tell me I haven't got it good."

Bensabat shook his head. "Yet you're desperate to be free. Slavery is a big pie supper all right. You misspelled *doubtless*." Bensabat pushed the flyer back across the counter with a "good day to you, son," and left the print shop.

The young pressman was still annoyed. "Damned Jew," he muttered, as he cranked the press back to life.

After the paper was bundled and out on the sidewalk for the delivery boys, Blanche locked up to leave for his job at the boarding house. He'd lied to Henry about why he was working the extra hours. He didn't have a dance to attend, though he wished he did. He was a little sweet on a girl his age, Sis, another of Henry's slaves, and he imagined it would be nice to take her to a dance. Most of his cash earnings came from overworking, serving food at Westport's best boarding house, but every dollar he earned went straight into Bensabat's strongbox.

He walked around the corner from the print shop and up a wide path that lead away from the town's commercial district. The boarding house was a residential hotel that served meals to its guests and anyone else with fifty cents who would mind his manners. The dining hall had tall ceilings. Lacy curtains graced the many windows. It was large enough to have dances for the churchgoing citizens of Westport. He imagined dancing there with Sis. It was her father, Reuben, whom Henry planned to sell, and Blanche worried about her while he lit the candles in the chandeliers overhead.

He served a supper of sweet potatoes, roasting ears, and fried chicken to patrons and guests at the boarding house. He kept his ears open to the dining room conversations. He never failed to learn something, and as a slave, he was invisible; the whites seemed to forget he was in the room and that he could hear everything they said. He was glad to have something to think about other than Reuben.

"Don't you think the secret handshakes and coded messages are little ridiculous?" The question was offered by Reverend Butler, a Methodist preacher, new to Westport. He didn't really expect an answer. "Blue Lodges. Ha! Preposterous, I should say."

Like every town in America, Westport was overrun with secret societies. Europeans needed government permission to join organizations, but white Americans had the right of free association. Clubs were springing up like wildflowers. The citizens of every state were in a "joining" frenzy. While they were eager to grow, the clubs excluded many prospective members: Indians, Jews, Irish, Italians, Catholics. Most of the groups had secret signs and symbols.

Another preacher, Scanlon, tried to change the subject. "Saint Paul told us the slave's duty is to serve his earthly master as he would serve his Christ."

"Earthly masters, I should say," said Phillips, a plump railroad lawyer stuffed into a satin vest. "Nothing but a low-caliber, bank-hating rabble."

At the far end of the table sat Colonel Lane and his wife Mary. Alongside them, the street orator, Stringfellow, drained a glass of whiskey. Stringfellow was a medical doctor and newspaperman who drank too much and could never understand why anyone would think slavery was wrong. He called his paper the *Squatter Sovereign*. He thought the name was funny and that an odd name would help him gain readers among the troublemakers who were squatting on Indian land. He reminded Blanche of his half-brother, the planter's so-called legitimate son, someone who didn't know how to live without slaves, incapable of putting on a clean shirt and tie by himself. Blanche supposed Stringfellow had a slave to dress him in the morning and clean him when he soiled himself. He drank so much, that probably happened all the time.

Arriving late, pushing other guests around as if they owned the place, were Stringfellow's compatriots: Atchison, Jones, and a big man named Thomason, who did most of the shoving. "Hey, boy. Another whiskey," Stringfellow bellowed, "and one each for my pals."

The preachers lit cigars at the political end of the table as Blanche served up whiskeys to Stringfellow and the late arrivals.

"What's the correct way to address a sheriff, anyway?" Atchison asked the others. "Your honor? Your highness?"

"I think it's *sheriff*," answered Thomason. He was a big hulk that tried everything he could to make the big shots like him.

"Aw shucks, we can do better than that. Hey, Preacher, let me introduce you to the next sheriff of Douglas County, Kansas, the soon-to-be-honorable, ahemmmm"—Atchison cleared an ever-present wad of phlegm from his throat—"Samuel Jones."

The innocent Reverend Butler took the bait. "I thought you were postmaster."

"I am," said Jones.

"I thought you were postmaster—here—in Westport."

"I am."

"And you're running for sheriff forty miles away? You moving?"

Jones grinned and elbowed Thomason in the ribs, reveling in Butler's confusion. "Nope. Hey, Preacher, come on and go with us to vote. I'll get you liquored up right smart."

The railroad lawyer couldn't help himself. "Hey, Jonesey," he chimed in, "I got a petition I've been pushing. Asks the territory legislature to let the voters use a secret ballot. They tried it in Australia. Worked out pretty good. How about you sign on?"

"Secret ballot?" Jones roared. "That may be all well and good for the Ostrich-alians, but in my mind if a man ain't enough of a man to voice his vote, he's got no business in the territory. You run your elections your way, I'll run mine my way."

4

— — —

Blanche trudged down a darkening lane with a heavy heart. *Surely Reuben knows about the sale already,* he lied to himself. *I won't have to be the one to break the news.* The young printer felt as if the weight of the world rested on his shoulders. He couldn't deceive himself. He knew he was the one who would have to break the bad news to Reuben.

Then clip-clop, clip-clop from behind him: two armed white riders. In the darkness of night, they looked like wraiths with no faces. He broke into a frightened run, but the horsemen overtook him as if his hob-nailed boots were trying to move through mud.

One spoke. "You stop when you see me, boy. You got that?"

"Let's see your pass," the other rider demanded.

Blanche showed the second horseman a slip of paper. His hand trembled. "He's okay," the rider croaked. "Get a wiggle in your git-along, boy."

Blanche sprinted toward a couple of one-room shacks. A group of slaves sat at a central campfire where Reuben was telling a stem-winder to Sis and his younger children. The storyteller was a big man, in his thirties. His wife, Sally, doctored fevered lash marks on his back as he talked. Reuben's defiance frequently brought him punishment. Blanche's chest heaved to catch his breath.

"Back on the Blue Ridge, the old folks tell about when Wolf cornered old Bobtail. Bobtail said, 'Wolf, you're strong and swift. But there's a creature whose powers have no match.'" Reuben stopped for a sip of water from a scoop fashioned from a hollowed-out gourd.

"Not the tar baby again," one of the children whined.

"Reuben, tell us a different one," Sally said. "We heard that one a hundred times." His four children stair-stepped in age and crowded around Sally, giggling, tickling one another, and spilling out across the ground. But the fun was over when they heard the telltale sound of clip-clop, clip-clop on the road. Blanche hadn't even had time to gasp out the warning.

The two armed horsemen stopped and surveyed the scene of the slaves at the campfire. They gloated over the discomfort they caused. Soon, with cruel smiles on their faces, they nudged their horses back to the road. As they disappeared into the gloom, the children ran into their parents' arms.

"Pattyrollers," said Reuben.

"I don't know why you keep calling them *patty-rollers*," said Blanche. "They're *patrollers*." He was being ornery, and he knew it. Maybe if he could pretend for a moment to dislike Reuben, it would be easier to share the bad news that he knew he had to tell.

"It's what I learned. It's what folks says."

Blanche's words were drenched with disdain. "Field hands say so, maybe."

"Yeah, I suppose." Long-suffering Reuben. He ignored Blanche's sharp, insulting words.

Sally was more indignant. "These childrens is scared plumb out of their skins." She and the little ones were calmed when Reuben began to hum a melody and then broke into song.

Some of these mornings bright and fair
Take my wings and cleave the air
Pharaoh's army got drown-ded
O Mary, don't you weep.

The oldest boy accompanied his father on a diddley bow, a single-stringed cigar-box banjo. It produced a swampy twang. The rest of the family joined in the chorus. Not Blanche.

O Mary, don't you weep, don't you mourn
O Mary, don't you weep, don't you mourn
Pharaoh's army got drown-ded
O Mary, don't you weep.

Well Mary wore three links of chain
On every link was freedom's name
Pharaoh's army got drown-ded
O Mary don't you weep.

When I get to Heaven goin' to put on my shoes
Run about glory and tell all the news
Pharaoh's army got drown-ded
O Mary don't you weep.

"Come on, Blanche," Reuben plead. "Ain't a gonna hurt you none to sing with us."

Sally encouraged one of the kids to sit in Blanche's lap. He pushed the child away. "Git off me. I ain't no one to you."

"Blanche, don't be so hard," Sis begged. She looked pretty tonight. He wanted to hold her hand and tell her everything was going to be all right.

"A man has got to be hard, Sis. So, here it is. I listened in on Marse Henry today. He's going to sell you, Reuben." Sharing the news didn't give Blanche an ounce of relief. His heart was still heavy.

Sally moaned with grief. They had not known.

The crackle of the campfire was the only other sound the slaves heard for a long minute. "I know'd it was coming." Reuben's words were brave, but his head hung in sadness. "Not near enough farm work around here to keep ol' Reuben busy. Ain't fit for cotton. Maybe he'll sell me to someone not so quick with the whip."

Now Sally's eyes burned as hot as the campfire. "Sis, get over here now."

All the children were bawling, even those too young to understand what was happening. A tearful Sis already gripped her mother's side. "Here I am, Mammy."

Sally untied a bandana from around her head. "Find every last gray hair you can and yank it out."

Sis wiped her eyes and went hard to work on the chore her mother laid out for her. It was difficult in the puny light of the campfire. "Just the gray ones, Mammy?"

"Just the gray ones, Sis. You leave those black ones where they are. You hear me?"

The smaller kids gathered around Blanche, and he pushed them away. "Go back to your Mammy. I got my hands full just taking care of myself. Damn kids."

"Why you have to always be a fusspot?" Sis scolded.

"Forgive him, Jesus," Sally prayed.

"And that's another thing. Damn all the churches and damn all the preachers. And damn all those Moses songs. It's nonsense. Killing an overseer and hightailing it out. I should say. It's crazy talk is all it is."

The faraway song of a bobwhite fell on the ears of the slaves. Then Reuben began singing again.

> *When the sun comes back and the first quail calls*
> *Follow the Drinking Gourd*
> *For the old man is waiting*
> *For to carry you to freedom*
> *If you follow the Drinking Gourd.*
> *The riverbank makes a very good road*
> *The dead trees will show you the way*
> *Left foot, peg foot, traveling on*
> *Follow the drinking gourd.*

"What you always singing that for?" Blanche asked. "You ain't going to run away."

"Gives me a little bit of peace to know how I'd go if I did take off."

"I suppose you think there really is an Underground Railroad," Blanche said, "and it's gonna spirit you off to freedom across that river."

"I'm sure of it."

"Tell you what. If the pattyrollers come sniffing around again, they'll find this fusspot in bed, right where he belongs. Watch me. Here I go. Chug, chug, chug. Look at me, I'm on the Underground Railroad."

Blanche thought Reuben was right. Maybe an Underground Railroad did exist. The East Coast newspapers said it did. But if he was going to make it through the night without breaking into tears himself, he needed to get away from Sis and the bawling babies. Mocking Reuben was just a good a way to end the conversation. He rose to his feet and stomped off, away from the campfire and toward one of the slave cabins.

5

— — —

The next morning, the muddy ditch through the middle of Westport bustled with townspeople, drovers, tradesmen, and pioneers. Every few minutes, a string of covered wagons rumbled past the print shop, loaded to the springs with goods and people headed west.

Blanche heard one of the passing settlers singing at the top of his lungs as his wagon passed Henry's print shop.

Oh don't you remember
Sweet Betsy from Pike
She crossed the great mountains
With her lover Ike
With two yoke of oxen
A big yeller dog
A tall Shanghai rooster
And an old spotted hog.

Paperboys jostled one another to be first in line as Blanche wrestled twine-bound bundles of newspapers onto the board sidewalk. An uproar down the block caught his eye.

What Blanche saw was that Williams had Reuben by the collar, and he was dragging him across the roadway. "No!" Reuben's voice choked through Williams's grip. Blanche dropped his bundles and ran to join the crowd that was gathering around the commotion.

Henry stood off counting a stack of gold coins. Then from nowhere, Sally, with her baby cradled in one arm, jumped into the fray. She managed to grasp Reuben's collar. She pulled him back to her. She couldn't free her husband, but she hoped perhaps she could slow Williams long enough to make him listen to her plea. The baby in her arms began to scream. Blanche scrambled to her side. "Come on, Sally, no good can come of this. Let it be."

Sally ignored him. "Oh! Master, master!" she cried. "Buy me and my children with my husband, Reuben, do, pray."

Without warning, Williams spun around and snatched a handful of Sally's hair. "How old you anyway, woman?"

"Twenty," Sally lied. "Just twenty years, Master."

Williams released his grip on Sally's hair. A smudge of soot blackened his palm.

"Twenty years, ha! You old nag." Williams was as mad as a sore-tailed bear. "Damn you, Henry. You think you can pull a fast one on me?"

Now Sally's children were crying out, "Mammy! Pappy!"

"Get back here, Sally," Henry shouted over the cries of the terrified children. "Blanche, get back to work."

But Sally continued to paw at Reuben and Williams, frantic, pleading, "Oh, master. Buy us all, do pray."

With the butt end of his carriage whip, Williams struck a sharp blow to the side of Sally's head. She fell to the ground, her bawling child still in her arms.

Now Henry rushed across the road, waving his arms and screaming like a banty rooster. "What you think you're doing, striking my slave woman?" He grabbed Sally's lifeless body. "Get up, Sally," he roared and then started to drag her back to her feet.

Reuben stooped to help Henry raise her up, but Williams pulled his whip handle across Reuben's neck. Reuben was powerless. His new master dragged him to the side of the road and attempted to shackle him to a wagon wheel. Without Reuben's help, Henry let Sally's body slump to the ground, limp as a ragdoll. Blanche fell to his knees beside her.

A woman's voice shrieked, "She's dead! She's dead!" Sally's baby, pinned beneath her mother's lifeless body, squalled like a pig under a gate.

With a great kick, Reuben shattered the wagon wheel and raced to Sally's side. "Oh my Sally! Oh Lord!"

Again Williams was on Reuben's back, trying to choke him to submission, but Reuben gathered himself, and spinning, threw a clenched fist at Williams's jaw. It met its mark. Williams stumbled backward and splattered into a barrel full of wooden tool handles in front of the general store. The barrel broke open and axe handles spilled across the sidewalk. Snatching one up, Reuben smashed Williams across the face and then chased him across the roadway toward Henry. As the panic-stricken crowd watched, Reuben cracked Henry hard across the neck with the axe handle. Henry crumbled to the ground in a heap.

Now the crowd grew angry. A black man had attacked not one but two white men. They'd seen it with their own eyes. The townspeople closed in on Reuben, but he held them at bay, swinging the bloodied axe handle overhead.

Blanche looked at the crowd. He was too frightened to run and fight at Reuben's side, and he was powerless to make him stop. Across the road, Williams lay on his side on the sidewalk, blood pumping from his nose. His face was a gory mess. He drew a pistol from his belt and shouted, "You!" Reuben twisted to face his master. Williams cocked back the pistol's hammer, pulled the trigger, and fired. The slug struck Reuben square in the forehead. He fell dead beside his wife, Sally. All Blanche could do was to take up the screaming child. He staggered back and tripped into a sitting position on the sidewalk, still cradling the baby in his arms. He choked back tears with quick, shallow breaths. His lips quivered. His eyes were riveted on Sis and the orphans and the bloody bodies sprawled across the roadway.

Sis pried the baby from Blanche's arms. Her siblings gathered around her, clinging to their sister's ragged dress. All of them were bawling. Tears as big as hedge apples rolled down their cheeks. Townspeople mobbed the fallen Henry. "Call for a doctor," a man's voice demanded.

"Save your breath," another man said.

Williams had propped himself on an elbow against a storefront. "Let the cheating bastard die." Then with a rattling cough, Williams's eyes rolled back in his head. His own words condemned him. Williams rolled off his elbow and into the slurry of the roadway, face down, stone dead.

Soon the crowd parted enough to allow passage to a long, narrow, high-wheeled cart. It was pushed by a gaunt man who was dressed in black and wore a tall black hat. The townspeople began to melt away, as if each of them was afraid he'd be enlisted to help the undertaker. Without ceremony, the gaunt man rolled Williams's body into a sitting position and lifted the body over his shoulder. He dropped the planter's carcass onto the cart as if it were a sack of beans.

Henry's body was next. Up and over the undertaker's shoulder, and then tossed in the cart. The dead bodies looked like two roasting ears lying side-by-side in the wagon bed. The undertaker shoved each gentleman's hat over his crushed face.

Now no one was in the roadway but the children and a few people with black faces. Two men picked up the bodies of Sally and Reuben. Women gathered Sis and the children and led them away. Blanche stumbled away. His heart was hollow. Henry had told him to get back to the print shop. That made as much sense as anything. Westport was silent.

6

— — —

The next day, Blanche idled away time on a creek bank. He tossed a pebble into the swift water. In the distance, in the corner of a meadow, Blanche could see a place where stones stood watch. It was Westport's graveyard. A small clutch of white mourners gathered near a pile of dirt and rock and a horse-drawn hearse. It was varnished shiny black and fitted with silver trim that glinted in the sun. Unless a family wanted to listen to a pack of screeching alley cats all night, it was best to bury the dead before the sun was allowed to set a second time.

The memorial service didn't have musical instruments. The mourners sang "Amazing Grace." Their voices were thin and strained, barely audible across the pasture.

> *Amazing Grace, how sweet the sound,*
> *That saved a wretch like me.*

I once was lost but now am found,
Was blind, but now I see.

Blanche walked farther down the creek. Beyond the place marked by the stones was a grove of wooden stakes. Strong black men leaned back against ropes and eased two crude wooden boxes into their final resting places. The graves were surrounded by other field hands—men, women and children—and the chorus of their song drifted on the wind, faint but full-throated.

If you get there before I do
Comin' for to carry me home,
Tell all my friends I'm comin' too,
Comin' for to carry me home.

Blanche walked into town and locked himself inside the print shop. Perhaps if he could work down the printing backlog, the images racing through his mind would go away. He turned the flywheel on the big press as if to print up a storm. But there was no paper. He hung his head. The sadness for Reuben and Sally began to fade. *I'm free now. I've still got money. Maybe I can buy Sis. God only knows what will become of those young'uns,* Blanche thought, then quickly scrubbed that idea from his head. *God doesn't care. God has nothing to do with it.* He turned the wheel and watched the empty press rock back and forth, madly clattering its lifeless story to no one but the musty print shop.

Blanche swept a pile of dust into the middle of the shop floor. He brushed the sweepings into a tray and dumped them in a trashcan. He swept the floor again. And again. He paced a circle path around the shop until finally, he found himself riveted in front of Henry's desk.

He remembered Reuben and Sally's mourners as they left the simple graveyard, their voices raised in songs of triumph and jubilation. The slaves and the preachers oftentimes talked about death as if it were a victory of some kind. The thought startled the young printer.

Victory. Henry's death is a sure-enough victory for me. I'm a freeman now.

He sat down in the publisher's chair, the one with a soft horsehair cushion that Henry never let him use. He found an apple that Henry had stashed in a side drawer, leaned back in the chair, put his feet on the desk, and took a satisfying bite.

Henry had never been overrun with friends, and Blanche thought some of the mourners came just to make sure for themselves that the printer was dead.

The widow had him help out at the house with the nosy callers, and now he eyed them one-by-one, wondering if Henry's death was a victory for any one of them. It took a couple of days for the widow to shed the house of her visitors. Blanche had to bide his time.

He was eager to talk to the widow, and as evening fell, two days after the burial, he found her sitting on the porch in Marse Henry's rocking chair, watching the roadway and listening to the night breeze whisper through the boughs of her shingle oak tree.

Widow Henry was a whale of a big woman. She wore a glossy black dress. The fabric seemed almost polished. It hid all but the toes of her shiny black button-up shoes and clutched tightly around her fleshy neck. A thin black lace necktie looked like it was trying to strangle her further, its tails draped down across her ample bosom. On top of her head, she wore a hat with a built-in veil, almost like a curtain, and she lifted back the veil continually so she could dab at her bloodshot eyes with a dainty black handkerchief. *As if she needs to remind folks that Marse Henry is gone*, Blanche thought. *She needs to go on stage with this act.*

"Your master left me a poor forsaken creature. Hardly a penny to my name."

"Oh, Missy, don't look at it that way. You got the print shop. You got some farm land. This house. And you got Reuben and Sally's kids. And Marse Henry, when he got himself pole-axed, he had a stack of gold that would sink a steamboat…"

"It's gone now. Everything. All we held dear. And two top-notch field hands. Dead and gone, just like that." The widow's tone now had an edge. "And them young'uns, nothing but four hungry mouths to feed. And you…why, look at you. Not much more than a child yourself. I can't put you out for enough wages to feed me, let alone you."

"No, Mistress, no you can't." Blanche waited for her eyes to draw down on him. "Because Marse Henry, he set me free."

The plump jowls of the widow shivered and pulled back. Her lips pursed into a scowl. "He never said anything to me about anything like that."

"Well, it's a fact. Put it in his will. He told me, 'Blanche,' he said, 'you're a freeman the day I put on that wooden overcoat.'"

"That fool." After she pulled at her nose and wiped across it with her handkerchief, her chin jutted out with defiance. "You can't be right," she said.

"Well, I am. But I'm willing to stay on for a spell. I can run that print shop for wages."

"Run it for me? Run the print shop for me?" The

widow looked around about the room as if to make sure no one was listening. "You can't run a print shop."

"Aw shoot, Mistress. Sure I can."

"They'd find out you can read. Folks would just as lief see you in prison."

"Prison? I'd have my freepapers." *Was the widow blind or insane?*

"Well, there's nothing of the kind in the strongbox."

"Let me see."

"I think not, and mind your impertinence."

"Mistress Henry, I'll stay on a couple of weeks, but after that we need to settle up accounts."

The widow balanced her ample carcass over the front edge of the rocking chair and, with a grunt, stood. She walked into the house. The door slammed in Blanche's face.

Blanche sat on the edge of the porch and listened to the south wind rustling in the top of the shingle oak. It was too early in the spring to hear the cicadas sing. *They'll know the truth when Henry's will gets read. A field hand might have to put up with double dealing but not me. No one trusts the Henrys. I have cash. I'll get a lawyer.*

"Blanche!" A stern voice carried to the porch from away, down roadway. It was Aunt Shoe Peg, the cook at the boarding house. She was a slave who had lost a leg below the knee after stepping on a nail. One of the kids said her wooden leg looked like the peg he hung his shoes on, and the name stuck. No longer fit for field labor, her master put her out to work for wages as a cook at the boarding house. "Where y'at? Son, you're late!"

Blanche ran as fast as his feet could carry him to the kitchen, a smallish shack a few steps outside the back door of the boarding house. The little shed seemed to ripple in the heat it threw off. He snatched a white apron from a clothesline and raced inside.

That evening's patrons collected into their favorite bunches. Blanche served the preachers and abolitionists at one end of the table and the pro-slavery gang at the other. Jones, Atchison, Stringfellow, and Thomason were joined by Colonel Lane and his wife. The banter of the slavers, fueled by whiskey, drowned out the chitchat of the genteel clergymen.

"Lane, when I'm sheriff," Jones roared, "I'll see to the law and leave the politics to you."

"That's big of you." Colonel Lane was grim and sober. Blanche once read that Colonel Lane had actually recruited two regiments of soldiers and led them into harm's way in the Mexican War, but he had the postmaster pegged as a whiskey-brave man who was all talk and no walk.

The slavers fell quiet once the victuals were served.

Colonel Lane broke the awkward silence as Blanche stepped in to clear away a try of dirty dishes. "Hear tell the Jayhawkers are gathering arms."

"Aw shucks," Jones said. "I stared eye-to-eye with the angel of death. A hunnerd times. Them coward Jayhawkers don't bother me none."

"Arumph." Atchison said, clearing his throat. "Don't you worry none about Jonesey."

"I guess we'll see," Colonel Lane said.

"We'll see, huh? Well what do you think of this?" Jones pulled back the lapels of this coat to reveal a rumpled waistcoat. He stuck his finger into a round hole four inches below his heart. "Huh? A Kaw chief done that, and he didn't live to tell the story!"

"Looks to me like that was more likely caused by a stray cigar ash." Colonel Lane's voice was playful, but his piercing eyes told another story. Jones's bluff had been called.

"Cigar ash!" Jones roared. He exploded to his feet, and tippling backward, he slammed into the waiter. Blanche and a tray full of dirty dishes crashed to the floor.

"Dang it, kid, watch where you're going!" Jones shouted.

At the same time, Atchison cleared his throat angrily, "Uh-huh-ahem," and Stringfellow slurred, "Clumsy damn…"

Tears welled in Blanche's eyes. "You can't talk to me like that. I'm free. It was his fault. Jones stumbled into me."

Thomason slowly stood and gingerly helped Jones return to his seat. "You're talking to your betters, boy."

Blanche was still on the floor, trying to pick up the broken dishes. "To hell with you. To hell with all of you. Why me?"

Thomason reached down and grabbed him by the collar. He swung a roundhouse at Blanche with a big beefy fist that connected and sent him flying across the room. The slavers laughed as if the sight was the funniest thing they'd ever seen.

"Let him be," Lane said. "He's just a kid."

Mrs. Lane averted her eyes. "Please," she said. "There are ladies present."

"This is men's business, Mrs. Lane," her husband told her with an icy stare. With that, Mary was on her feet, scurrying from the room, pressing a handkerchief to her lips.

Thomason snatched Blanche up by the belt and collar and, to a chorus of laughter, ran him out of the dining room and to the back door of the boarding house. He threw Blanche out through the back door as if he were a sack of dirty rags.

"They're laughing at you, you big clown," Blanche said. He regretted his words. Thomason hit him again, and he rolled up against the wall of the kitchen.

"No one laughs at me," he said. The big man removed his belt and flogged Blanche across the back—again and again, a dozen times—before saying, "Now maybe you'll know how to treat your betters." He returned inside with a smile, delighted to have shown his friends that he was superior to someone.

The sounds that rolled out of the boarding house were jovial. Slavers and preachers alike, they all seemed indifferent to whether or not Blanche survived his beating. That stung him almost as bad as the welts across his back.

He dragged himself into a sitting position against a tree. He dabbed at the bloody cuts on his face with the tail of his apron. *Forget it, Blanche. You fool.*

A cloudy night sky smothered light in the back alley of Westport. After a deep breath, Blanche rose to his feet and threw off his apron. On the weary trudge to his cabin, he thought, *If Henry ever did make me out a freepaper, even if it shows up, that widow won't let me go free without a fight.* He stopped in his tracks and retraced his steps to the backdoor of Bensabat's house.

He rapped his knuckles on the jamb of Bensabat's back door. No answer. Again. Bensabat, in his nightclothes, stuck his head out the door and looked back and forth at his neighbors' houses. Sometimes Blanche thought that the whites spent every evening watching each other through their nightshades.

"I'm needing my cash," Blanche told him, his tears mixed with blood and mucous from his nose.

"Are you all right?"

"I'll live."

"Give me a minute." Bensabat returned with a fat leather wallet and handed it over to Blanche.

"I think the widow will sell," says Blanche.

"The print shop?"

"No. Me."

"She'll ask plenty."

"Why don't you buy me? I'll work for you. I'll work it off."

"I wish I could…but no. My people…we were slaves once too."

Blanche rubbed his throbbing lip.

Blanche washed his face in a bucket before entering the rear of the Henry home. He found the widow sitting in the dark on the front porch.

She ignored him until he said firmly, "What do you figure me to be worth, anyway?"

"I don't know." The widow's voice was tentative. Then she turned to face him. "Fifteen hundred maybe."

"Fifteen hundred?"

"A good house servant…I've heard fifteen hundred plenty of times."

"I can give you one hundred eighty right now. And I can pay you twenty a month for five years. Now that's about a thousand, and I figure that's way more than top dollar."

"Sorry. I can do better. Have my breakfast ready at eight. Then we'll go over to the print shop. See what's there. Eight o'clock sharp."

Blanche's hands knotted into fists.

"And let's get one thing straight. I won't abide that high hat talk out of you. I'm not Mr. Henry."

7

— — —

Reuben's little ones sat with Sis on a bench across the campfire from Blanche. He stared into the licking flames, haunted by the widow's words. He heard them over and over. *Folks would just as lief see you in prison.*

He picked up a stick of firewood. Long and slender, like an axe handle. His hand felt along the length and caressed the straight grain. *Folks would just as lief see you in prison.*

Blanche gripped the heavy rod with both hands at the end and then angrily smashed it into the coals of the campfire. The children screamed and scurried for cover. Embers flew high into the dark night sky and caught on the south wind, drifted north, toward the muddy Missouri River. The clouds above were breaking. The stars in the Big Dipper emerged, the same cluster of stars that Reuben always called the Drinking Gourd.

"Forks on the left. Always serve butter on a butter plate." The widow was still in her nightdress and kerchief. She sat in up bed. As Blanche laid a tray of food across her lap, a napkin slipped from the tray and fell to the floor. Under the bed was a wide ceramic pot that the widow evidently used if nature called during the night. Folks called pots like that a thunder mug. Beside it, Blanche saw a strongbox. He thought he saw a snarl on her lip when he stood to serve her.

As the noontime hour approached, Blanche swept and boxed loose ends in the print shop. The widow sat in Henry's chair at his roll-top desk. Blanche hoped it would break under her weight. She was dressed in black, all the way from her flabby turkey neck to the floor. She'd set aside her veil when she'd first arrived and spent the morning with her nose buried in Henry's business ledgers.

Blanche lost himself in his thoughts. He swept the same pile of dust from place to place. All his problems would be solved if he could just find those freepapers. He schemed, thinking of ways he could look for them in Henry's house. He heard, "Folks would just as lief see you in prison" and startled.

"Did you say something to me?" he asked the widow.

"Not a thing."

He must have imagined it. He didn't like the way she glared at him now. He tried to redirect her attention. He started, indicating the ledger she'd just cracked open. "That book shows who owes—"

"Did he let those ruffians out of here without paying for the ballots?"

"He got money, cash on the barrelhead."

"There's not a receipt."

"He wrote everything down but gave the receipt to them. That's how it works. They keep the receipt to prove..." Her blank stare told him he may as well have been talking to the wall. She didn't understand the business at all.

The widow glared at Blanche and snapped the ledger closed. "I'll be back after lunch." She donned her black-veiled hat and tucked a parasol under her arm along with the ledger.

Before the widow had crossed the road, Blanche grabbed his canvas newspaper bag and exited the back of the shop. With one eye on the widow, he stole across the roadway, hidden behind a mule, to block the widow's view. Now he was away and running down an alley. He ran as fast as he could, past the Methodist church where a sign in the yard read, *NORTHERN METHODIST EPISCO-PALIAN CHURCH. REV. PARDEE BUTLER PRESIDING.*

Blanche ran on toward the edge of town. He slowed when he began to feel a stitch in his side, under the canvas bag, and he took the opportunity to peek out of an alleyway between storefronts. He was nearer now to the Henry house than the widow, ahead of her by at least a couple of hundred yards.

When he looked again, what he saw was that the widow's progress had slowed to a standstill. A commotion was taking place in the road in front of the Methodist church.

As Blanche ran on, the widow stood aside to watch Atchison, Stringfellow, and Thomason molest Butler, the Methodist preacher. They had Butler surrounded. The ruffians pushed and shoved him between themselves, knocking off his hat, tearing his clothes. Thomason menaced him with a Bowie knife. Stringfellow twisted and pinched his flesh. Not a soul on the roadway was brave enough to defend Butler from the oversize brute Thomason, and outnumbered, three-on-one, Butler was unable to defend himself.

But he was able to break away. He ran to the sanctuary of his church house only to find the postmaster, Jones, driving sixteen-penny nails through the door and into the jamb, nailing the door closed. "This church house has been closed. Everlastingly. By order of me."

Butler sank to his knees as if to pray. It was God's house. This was America. A thousand protests must have raced across his mind, but, crestfallen, all he could only say was "You can't get away with this."

Jones shouted loud enough for everyone in Jackson County to hear. "When we get back from Kansas, every last one of them nails had better by God still be in place."

Across the roadway, Butler's friend Scanlon swept the vestibule steps at another religious sanctuary. The marquee beside the door read, *SOUTHERN METHODIST CHURCH*. His face, twisted into a fearful frown, looked across the road at his friend Butler.

"What the hell you looking at?" Thomason bellowed at all the denizens of Westport in general and at Scanlon in particular.

With grins stretched across their faces, Jones and Thomason turned on Scanlon. They took brisk strides in his direction. When Thomason raised his Bowie knife again, Scanlon shook his head, threw aside his broom, and scurried into his church. He set the lock behind him.

"Every last nail." Thomason brayed like a mule. "You hear the man?" Thomason and Jones mounted horses they'd left hitched in front of Scanlon's church.

Atchison and Stringfellow rode alongside in a buckboard. Together, the slavers rode west, out of town and into the prairie beyond. Self-satisfied smiles spread across their faces.

The widow Henry resumed her walk home. She supposed that Butler had it coming. A lot of people had it coming in Westport; her recently deceased husband had always said that was so, and she was too busy tending to her own concerns. She needed to figure out how to squeeze some money out of what remained of the print shop.

She averted her eyes so as not to have to look at the hang-dog preacher kneeling at the stoop of his church house. The tragedy of her own personal loss was far more important to her than the misadventure of one pitiful preacher.

Blanche ran to the rear entrance of the Henry house and let himself in. He peeked between the lace curtains in the parlor to see if anyone was watching. The air he drew into his lungs seemed as thick as syrup. He couldn't catch his breath, and his heartbeat pounded in his ears like a kettledrum. He scampered up a narrow stair.

Blanche heard the whinny of a horse outside. Then voices. Once inside the bedroom, he checked the street again for the widow's progress, but was unable to see her.

He bounced across the bed and reached underneath for the strongbox. It's wasn't where it had been before. He reached again. Nothing. He flopped on the floor. His hand found the strongbox hidden behind the widow's thunder mug, and he pulled it into the sunlight.

The locks on the box held tight. Blanche's eyes searched the room for a tool. Nothing. Not on the mantle of the fireplace, not in the hearth. Only a pile of burned scraps of paper lay on the bricks. He knew what that was: papers that the widow didn't want anyone to see. *If I had known she'd do this…*he said to himself. He crushed the ashes into dust, wishing he had the widow's flabby neck in his hands instead.

Blanche heard a door open and shut downstairs and then the creaking sound of floorboards under stress. *If there are any freepapers, they're in that box,* he told himself. He couldn't risk staying another second. He raised a window sash, gathered up the box into his canvas bag, and scooted out onto the roof, closing the window once he was outside.

He jumped from the roof and rolled across the turf to deaden his fall. With the strongbox hidden in his newspaper pouch, Blanche followed the alley back to the storefronts of Westport, whistling a tune, as if his papers had all been peddled.

Hiding under the counter at the print shop, Blanche pried apart the hinges of the strongbox with a screwdriver. Inside was a document written in longhand titled *LAST WILL AND TESTAMENT*. It was dated 1848, long before Henry had acquired his property interest in Blanche. Blanche was no railroad detective, but after finding the ashes in the widow's hearth, it was as plain as the big fat nose on the widow's fat face that she'd burned her husband's most recent will.

"Damn you, Henry. I don't know who's worse, you or your wife." He would never have forgiven himself for not finding out what was in the box, but now that he had the box, it was a problem. It was evidence of his theft. He would have to dispose of it somehow. After hiding the strongbox under a pile of refuse, he stepped out behind the shop and vomited.

Blanche sat in a corner of the print shop and was finishing off a piece of corn pone when the widow Henry returned. The cornmeal disk was a dry as a buffalo chip, and he hoped he could keep it down. After this lunchtime escapade, even water would have tasted dry.

"Get yourself up. I don't have time for you to

lollygag around. Let's see some work out of you for a change."

Blanche grabbed his broom and swept again, his eyes glued to the floor. Later, under a heavy brow, he lifted his eyes to take a long look at his mistress. *She must have that ledger memorized by now.* He wished that he didn't have to see her.

He wished he could straighten out the twisted metal box and return it to its hiding place behind the widow's chamber pot, but it was too late for that. She would find out that he had taken it. She would never train him as a house servant now. He knew that he would never again see the inside of the widow's house. He'd be beaten and auctioned off. His options were narrow now, all because he stole the strongbox. He should never have taken it. He should have waited for another opportunity.

The idea of running away intruded on his thoughts again and again that afternoon. He didn't want to run away, and he tried to think of other things. Running away was stupid. Hopeless. He thought about Sis, then realized he was thinking about his mother as well, how because of slavery, someone he was close to could be lost even without running away. All the widow had to do was put Sis on the auction block, which she might just do anyway because Sis had the additional burden of the young'uns. Sis and the young'uns wouldn't be in Westport at the end of the summer, he convinced himself of that.

Henry's old biddy would never be able to make a go of the printing business. She'd need to hire a printer. A white man's salary would gobble up all the profits. Even then, she'd need someone to keep his ear to the ground for all the town gossip and news stories, someone clever enough to twist the truth to suit the merchants and slave owners.

No, the old cow was fixing to lose her shirt. She might think the past-due customers would pay up, but even Blanche knew that was a false hope. Henry's customers would only pay for last week if they needed an ad for next week. Trying to collect those old debts would be about as fruitful as farting at a whirlwind. Blanche knew that, but she would never listen to him. She'd be lucky to get ten dollars from chasing down deadbeats. She was broke. She just didn't know it yet.

Even if she didn't sell him off for stealing the strongbox, the widow wouldn't have any choice once she realized she was broke. Just like him. Out of choices. Any way she jumped, the widow was going to wreck all of his plans for the future. If he let her settle on her way, then the best he could look forward to was a life of chopping cotton.

He had no promise of thinking his next master would be as enlightened as Henry. Reading and books would only get him a good thrashing. He lost all hope. *I just want to die,* he told himself. *That would be better than laboring under the whip, bent over in the sun, just to earn a dollar for another man.* His throat was as tight as old Dick's hatband. His nose began to run and tears burned his eyes.

Blanche stewed over his plight all afternoon and narrowed down his choices to two. He could run away, and if caught, he'd take a beating from the slavecatcher and then again from the widow. He couldn't count on a warm homecoming from her because she would have to cough up a bundle for the reward money that she would owe the slavecatcher. Then he would have to wait for the inevitable day when he was sold down the river.

Or he could just wait. Take a whipping for stealing the strongbox, watch the widow go broke, and then get sold down the river. The choice was stark. At least if he ran away, he'd have a chance, not a good chance, but if any of those stories about an Underground Railroad were true, he did have a slim chance, and that was better than none. A chance to be free and use what he'd learned to better himself, to rise above being just another cottonpicker like Reuben had been.

He felt some remorse now, remorse for the times he had mocked the poor soul. A life of suffering, threatened daily by vengeance for the slightest mistake. Reuben had only wanted to be sold with his family, a simple kindness, but that was the way of slavery. His life had been a well of sorrow, like Blanche's mother's had been. That's all Blanche had to look forward to, the day when he had to go to work in the fields. That day he was sure was right around the corner.

A growing anger ate at his insides now. He didn't fear the loss of his friends. He'd worked hard to learn to read, and he had ached for freedom long before Henry surrendered his soul to the Almighty. Henry was good for something after all. His death opened the door, but then the widow slammed it in his face. If he'd only seen this coming, he could have hidden Henry's will. Now all his plans to become a master printer were dashed. He wouldn't get his freepapers. No walking down the sidewalk saying "howdy do" to whomever he wanted. No reading a book when he felt like it. *Yes, Marse overseer, let ol' Blanche chop another row. Sho' nuff, Marse overseer, let Blanche get you a cool sip of water.* He wanted to vomit again. *It would all be so different if Henry had just told me to write out my freepapers.* In that moment, his nausea passed. He had a plan.

As evening approached, Blanche lugged a heavy box of trash out the back door. His cash was in a wallet on his hip, and the rocky, brush-choked creek below looked inviting, but he had one more task. When he returned, the widow snapped up the ledger and gathered her hat and parasol.

"Mistress, you remember I overwork at the boarding house…?"

"As long as I get my breakfast at eight, suit yourself." The doorbell rang as the widow pulled the front door of the shop closed behind her.

Blanche wrote out a document in longhand. In large capital letters, across the top, he wrote, *BLANCHE KELSO BRUCE FREEPAPERS.*

Blanche Kelso Bruce Freepapers, Independence, Missouri, June 7th, 1854.

This to make known to all whom it may concern, that Blanche Kelso Bruce the bearer of this paper, is a free boy. He was put with me having learned the Carpenters trade in Sedalia. He lived with me Some Six years. I have universally found him to be Strictly honest and Strictly observes the truth, has never been put much to Joining Carpenter work, but is very good at trying up timber and preparing ready for joining in framing, has always been Serviceable particularly in mortising for Sash panel doors &c. As to his freedom there is no question of that. I know his Mother & sister.

Edward H. Henry Esqr

Morgan Payne formerly of Sedalia is in possession of his freepapers.

Morgan Payne, Recorded the 17th June, 1854

Blanche forged signatures on the emancipation, comparing Henry's signature on his old will and then rocked a pad across the document to absorb any wet ink. He folded and stuffed the document into his wallet. After locking the front door of the print shop, Blanche set the lock on the rear door, stepped across the threshold, and pulled it shut behind him.

He ran south. Before he'd gone far, brush along a rocky creek gave him cover. He waded across and then turned west, upstream, into the prairie, running toward the sinking sun.

8

— — —

As night fell on the prairie, Blanche followed the south bank of the rocky creek west. The Big Dipper appeared in the night sky, off to his right, as soon as it was dark. The night was cloudless. The crisp air in his lungs freed him from fear. All he could think about was putting the maximum amount of distance between himself and Westport. His mind blocked out the sounds of the prairie night. He wouldn't have heard a wildcat if it screeched in his ear, but he would have heard the telltale clip-clop of mounted pattyrollers.

He guessed it must have been midnight when the brook took a turn toward the south and up a rise. That was the end of the creek. Its headwater was a spring that dribbled out of a rocky outcrop.

Blanche continued walking toward the south. He reasoned that if anyone came looking for him, they would naturally guess he took off to the north, toward the free states. Aside from that, he was reluctant to choose north on no more authority than the words in a campfire song. What he did believe was the talk of white men in such matters: Henry always said that Osawatomie, sixty or so miles to the south, was filthy with Jayhawkers, and boarding house chatter gave even more reasons to recommend it. Eventually he'd turn north, toward Detroit, maybe, eventually, Canada. Toronto.

For the most part, abolition folks stood firm against violence of any sort. They thought of themselves as peacemakers, not fighters, cut from the same bolt of cloth as the Anabaptists and Quakers. But Blanche had heard quite a different story at the boarding house. Folks said a group of abolition men in Osawatomie, led by a wiry old Yankee named John Brown, was shipping in arms and eager to make a war.

He felt the ground under his feet falling away just a smidgen and guessed that he'd left high ground and headed down another watershed.

Trees began to appear at intervals. He could see them outlined by stars, but after more weary hours of trudging, he noticed that the sky was brightening from the east. The going was beginning to get tough. The grass was thicker, and the ground below his feet was nothing but mud. He could hear the far-off chattering of ducks.

Blanche found a tree with low limbs and climbed up to a crook twenty feet above the ground.

Ahead of him, he could see a wetland. It seemed boundless, like looking into a mirror at a mirror. It disappeared into itself in someplace beyond. Once, a bird hunter had told Aunt Shoe Peg about the Marais Des Cygnes, the marsh of the swans, and how big it was. "I'll take that with a dose of salt," she told him. "Tell me something I can believe." And then they were back to haggling over the price she'd pay for a brace of geese he'd killed.

Blanche had not imagined that a stream could reach beyond the horizon. His problem was that Osawatomie was somewhere on the other side. It made little difference that Blanche couldn't swim. He could see in the breaking dawn that the place was more of a bog than a marsh—too shallow to swim anyway, too muddy to walk across. A boat would be useless, even if he had one.

Blanche shinnied down from the tree to mull over his choices. He couldn't continue south because of the marsh. East would take him back to Westport. If anyone went looking for him, they would look north. A westward track would only take him farther into the wilderness. So he decided his best advantage was to get back to drier ground and then bear north and west.

He was delighted by his choice. The upturned face of the prairie in the glow of morning sun was painted with wildflowers. Every minute that passed brought the song of a meadowlark to Blanche's ear. A steady southeast breeze pushed him forward. Tired though he was, a big smile covered his face. He had no fear. He was a needle in the world's largest a haystack. He sang songs, and when that left him breathless, he whistled.

In the past, on occasion, he sometimes doubted his choices. Aunt Shoe Peg had often teased him for having difficulty making up his mind. She said he stewed himself in his own juice. If he walked to the print shop on the north side of the road, likely as not, he'd worry about not walking on the south side. He would sometimes put on his red tie, take it off and put on the blue tie, worry a spell, then put the red tie on again. Not today. He was proud to be a runaway.

Always before, when planning for his future, he had nixed the idea of running away, but now he realized that running away was the right decision, the best decision for him, and he couldn't think of a single reason to second-guess his choice. He was getting awfully tired and hungry, but he was also downright self-satisfied.

Maybe he'd start his own newspaper. He could almost imagine the masthead, trumpeting the news:

"Blanche Bruce Ran Away—So Can You!" Then he remembered Sis and the young'uns, and his thoughts became clouded with the realization that even if fortune smiled on them and *The New York Times* sent a boy to deliver the paper to their doorstep every day, they still wouldn't be able to read it.

The tallgrass prairie was a land without shadow. It was dominated by big bluestem grass that stretched farther in every direction than Blanche could see. A sea of grass, folks said. The few trees on the prairie were stunted and crouched low in ravines. The wind rippled across the big bluegrass like waves on a pond. Last years' growth stood tall and in clumps, colored a pale orange. Alongside, waist-high slender spikes of this year's grass sprang out of the earth. In another couple of months, new growths of grass would mature to the characteristic blue-purple, and in spots, the bluestem spikes would reach eight feet in height. But this early in the spring, none of the three-spiked seed heads had yet emerged that gave big bluestem its common name, turkeyfoot.

The runaway found himself on top of an east-west ridge. Across it, a trace led southwest. It was littered with broken jars, boxes, and furniture. He knew he was crossing the Santa Fe Trail. It led to the high desert territory, New Mexico, and was wide, as wide as a city block or more, and on it, the prairie grass was beaten down to stubble. Only a couple of years before Blanche was born, Santa Fe had been part of Texas, after Colonel Lane and the American army took it from Mexico in one of Henry's favorite wars. His young printer never thought to question it.

Blanche stopped in his tracks and looked around. The sun was warmer and the air sweeter. The songs of the meadowlarks were more vibrant. He felt a tingling in his legs and looked down at his feet, then turned to look behind himself. He thought for a moment that the sensations that were washing over him had something to do with the prairie grass or the lonely westward trail. He stamped his foot on the ground. It was pretty much the same as the soil in Westport and no different than the way he remembered that it had been in Virginia. Then he realized, *This is the first time I've ever set my foot on free soil.* His heart leapt in his chest. What Blanche felt was something he'd never felt before. Joy. He wished his mother was at his side.

9

— — —

The thick grasses made walking difficult. Blanche swung wide to avoid getting close to a couple of places it looked like folks had settled. *Not a tree in sight,* he thought, but then he saw, a couple of miles in the distance, a small grove of trees trying to make the best of it, and as he walked nearer, he could see the banks of a creek. He could just see beyond a bend, on the north bank, an outcropping of stone. *Greenhorn.* He remembered the name Henry and the nesters back in Westport gave to the abundant local stone. But as he tramped nearer, Blanche realized the white patch ahead was not a cluster of sun-bleached stone but a farmhouse and barn.

He thought for a moment he smelled Auntie Shoe Peg's ham hock and beans but then realized the wind was blowing on his back, toward the farm. His mind conjured up a picture of a bowl of ham hock and beans again, and it didn't matter if the smell was real or not. The growling in his stomach was real. The wind must have carried his scent across the divide, because now he heard a dog barking.

The farm sat beside a road that Blanche didn't see until he was almost on top of it. Chickens pecked at grasshoppers in the yard. A cat stalked prey at the edge of the tallgrass. A quilt hung from the sill of a window.

Beside the campfire, it had been easy to act as if the Underground Railroad was a dream. Blanche would never be in a position to know, anyway. And he reinforced this thinking with the lies he had to tell his master. Henry had asked him about it a few times, and Blanche had told him that he didn't know anything but campfire big talk that nobody but a fool would believe in. He didn't tell Henry about the articles he'd read in *The New York Times*. Henry didn't need to know he'd been reading someone else's newspaper, and a Yankee paper at that.

But now…Sally had repeatedly said that a conductor could signal his whereabouts with the wagon wheel quilt. That was supposed to be a secret. He didn't know what to think. Sally and Reuben told lots of things at the campfire and most of it was bunk. But ahead, a quilt hung out the window for everyone to see, and on it was the design the women called wagon wheel.

When he thought about it, Blanche didn't remember ever seeing a quilt hanging out in the elements. They took hundreds of hours to make; most of that the quilters spent hunkered over in the dim light of a fireplace or lantern. Rich folks had coal oil, but the light cast from lanterns wasn't much of an improvement over a campfire. After nightfall, even the dining hall of the boarding house was dimly lit. Maybe the treasured handiwork was hanging out the window for a reason. Maybe it was meant to send him a message. He was tired and hungry, no maybe about that.

The farmer's dog barked and growled as he got closer, but the only growling Blanche paid any attention to was that in his stomach. He approached the back door, mustered up his courage, and knocked on the jamb.

A woman opened the door a crack. "What do you need?" she asked, and with that, she kicked the door open wide and backed away. She wasn't much taller than Blanche and must have been twice his age. She wore a long dress that was high around her neck and reached to the floor below her. The stock of a long rifle jammed into her shoulder, and she stared down the barrel with a blank expression. The gun sight pointed straight at Blanche's chest. Her face was flat—she seemed to have no cheekbones or brow.

Blanche stepped back. "Good day, Missus. You have any work for a traveling man?"

"Don't get any ideas—my husband is just out behind the barn."

Blanche didn't believe her husband was behind the barn, not for a minute. "I don't have any ideas, Missus, except maybe I could do a day's work and maybe get a plate of food." He desperately wished he could eat first, but he knew there had to be a trade and that the prairie woman held all the cards.

She looked unforgiving. She never lowered the rifle stock from her shoulder. "If I was to break a leg," she told Blanche, "not a living soul would slap a drop of whitewash on that chicken coop. The makins is in the barn." With that, she slammed the door shut with her toe.

Blanche ran as fast as he could toward the barn. *Better not give her a chance to change her mind*, he thought.

Blanche found a bucket of lime and another of chalk in the barn. He mixed them together with dirty water from a trough in the yard, found a brush and a big straw hat, and soon hard at work slopping the whitewash on the chicken coop. Tillis had taught him how to make it, and the work helped him forget the ache in his belly. The shack was made of rough sawn planks that drew up the moisture from the whitewash, so Blanche slapped it on thick. It would be several days more before the whitewash showed any sign of drying.

As midday approached, the stomach growling started again. His throat was parched.

Blanche found the farm's water well beside the water trough. The farmer had set flat flagstones around a hole in the ground and covered the hole with a plank of wood. Below ground, the well was at least four feet across. The sides were stacked stones. A few feet below the surface, the well was pitch black. A three-legged structure stood over the well, and where the legs met at the top, the farmer had secured a wheel. Strung up over the wheel was a rope and on the end of the rope, a bucket. Blanche played the bucket down the well.

Blanche knew the bucket had reached the bottom when the rope went slack. Now he pulled on the rope, and the weight told him that the bucket was full. It was heavy. Hand over hand, he strained to withdraw the bucket from the well. When it reached the surface, he tipped most of the contents into the trough, it was so heavy, but saved enough to quench his thirst.

He struggled to drink from the bucket. He was like an ant drinking from a giant's glass. The dog began barking, and Blanche tipped the bucket higher. The last bit of water rushed out and overflowed his mouth, splashing down on his shirt.

He laughed. He couldn't remember the last time he'd laughed, and it felt good. Then, far away to the southeast, down the road, Blanche spotted riders. *No wonder he's barking.* Nearer now, he could make out a light wagon and two horsemen.

"Missus!" he yelled.

The farm wife came to the door, wiping her hands on her apron. "What is it?"

"Missus, looks like you got company."

Blanche recognized the party as customers from the boarding house: Jones, Atchison, Stringfellow, and Thomason. Each wore a short white ribbon tied into a buttonhole. The color told other folks that the wearer was pro-slavery.

Blanche sprinted back to the chicken coop and picked up his bucket of whitewash. "Missus, if I was you, I'd get your rifle. Quick." He pushed the straw hat on his head and shoved the brush into the pail. He allowed his hand to immerse in the whitewash. Then the other hand. He rubbed some on his face.

As the travelers approached the farm house, Blanche worked his way sideways, on around back of the coop, wary to avoid any quick movements and careful to keep the back of the straw hat turned toward the riders.

The travelers dismounted their horses and wagons near the well and allowed their horses to drink from the trough. They drew water from the well and filled canteens as Blanche painted his way around the corner of the coop. He peered out from the far side.

The farmer's wife toed open the door. The stock of her rifle was planted firmly in her shoulder. "You got business here?"

"Gonna have an election, I hears," Jones said.

"Wouldn't know. It's the men folks that vote, not women." Nodding in the direction of the horses gulping water from the trough, she said, "Did you ever think of asking?"

Atchison chimed in. "You mind if we water the horses, ma'am?"

"Let 'em have their fill. Then keep moving."

"Haven't seen no fugitive slaves, I don't reckon?" Jones asked.

"See to your stock and then git." She pulled back the rifle's hammer with a loud click. She meant business.

Behind a corner of the chicken coop, Blanche kept a steely eye on the travelers, particularly Thomason, the bully who had given him the beating. He felt a dull, throbbing pain surge through the welts on his back. He imagined it was caused by his blood boiling, but more than likely, it was because the sun was beating down on his shoulders.

Stringfellow dismounted the buckboard and led his horse to the trough. "I don't know how a man could expect to improve his property in a place like this without slaves."

"Let me know next time you take a piss, pretty boy," Jones said. "I'll have Thomason help you."

Thomason bristled.

"We got an election to win," Atchison said. "You all can finish this later."

What buffoons, Blanche thought. To him, String-fellow and Atchison were fools, but he'd like to throw a set of shackles on Jones and Thomason, just to see how they liked it.

Soon enough, the travelers loaded up with an "Appreciate your hospitality, ma'am." They turned out of the barnyard and onto the road, which now bent due north. None of them seemed to have noticed that behind the straw hat, the chicken coop painter was a boy with whitewash smeared on his face, snow-white forearms, and menacing eyes.

Blanche washed the whitewash off his arms as the sun faded into the western sky. The whitewash had enough lime in it to burn his flesh if he left it long. His stomach growled again. He bathed his face in the grubby water, and clearing his eyes, he saw a plate of food. Right under his nose. A wide smile split across the farm wife's rawhide face.

"Bless you, Missus." Blanche wolfed the food.

"Slow down. There's plenty more where that come from."

"Are you…?"

"What, son?"

He wanted to ask her if she was a conductor on the Underground Railroad. But he figured if he himself was a conductor, he'd deny it to the last ditch. She might even get the wrong idea and think he was a detective. "Never mind."

Nothing was to be gained by making her fess up, and he wouldn't want any trouble that came his way to fall back on her. She'd treated him with kindness. At least now, some of his doubts were resolved. From all indications, the Underground Railroad was a reality.

Blanche spread prairie hay into something like a pallet on the floor of the barn. He hadn't slept at all the night before, but he had a full belly and so he dozed off quickly. It seemed like only moments later that he was stirred awake by the farmer's wife. She was bringing him a dish towel full of food. "Clear and sunny. A great day the Lord has given us."

"I can't thank you enough, ma'am."

"There's a conductor in Lawrence. Be on the lookout for a lantern that burns at high noon. I'd steer clear of the road if'n I was you."

Blanche drank deeply from the bucket at the well. The farmer's wife handed him a flour sack filled with hoe cakes and a ketchup bottle filled with clean water. "The Lord be with you, son," she prayed.

With a "Thanks again, Missus," he was off into the prairie, angling a bit further west every time the road came into view.

Blanche tromped through the tallgrass prairie all day, until night overtook him. He was so weary he didn't think he could take another step, but he did manage to walk in a circle to tread down a bed of grass. Before falling asleep, he pointed his ketchup bottle, already drained of its water, toward the North Star. *If it's cloudy when I wake up, at least I'll know which way is north.*

10

— — —

All Blanche heard was the sound of a steady breeze rustling over the tallgrass and the song of meadowlarks. The morning had broken. The sky above was full of small, puffy clouds, driven north on the wind. *Like popcorn,* Blanche thought, and his stomach growled. He ate a hoe cake, but then his mouth was as dry as a bone. He chewed on a stalk of grass for the tiniest bit of moisture.

Blanche stood on tiptoes to take bearings. The sun played peek-a-boo behind the clouds, so he searched the horizon in the direction his ketchup bottle told him was north. Grass, farther than he could see. Nothing but grass and wildflowers. Behind him too, and to either side, grass. Green, gold, red, white. In the distance, where the splotchy shadows from the windblown clouds danced across the rippling prairie, the land looked almost purple.

The wind pushed harder against his back this day. It was warm and moist. By midday, the breeze had driven the puffy clouds beyond the northern horizon. Only the tips of high, wispy clouds fingered their way into the sky above the prairie to the northwest.

By midafternoon, Blanche was thirsty, hungry, hot, and soaked with sweat. He cursed the sun. The turkeyfoot grass was so thick that walking was a chore, and the south wind was whipping it into a frenzy.

He was gladdened to come upon a tiny rivulet of water. After drinking and refilling his bottle, he sat back and rested. An image of a preacher filled his senses, and Blanche looked around to find himself front and center at Sunday services. The preacher was in the pulpit looking straight down at him, and he repeatedly slammed the Good Book into the lectern. Blanche knew he was dreaming.

He didn't sleep long, and he awoke unrefreshed. The dream had him unsettled. He took a final drink and launched himself north again, pushed along by the wind. The high, wispy clouds now filled the northwest sky and threatened to block the sun. He heard the sound of low, rumbling thunder in the distance and knew now why his sleepy mind had conjured up the image of a Bible-banging preacher.

Before he could cross the next low rise, the cloud-bank overtook the daylight. Backlit by the sun, the thin, high clouds looked like a golden halo on the head of a heavier bank of clouds that darkened the sky below. The northwestern horizon disappeared, and the peals of thunder sounded less distant. The wind whipped and raced across the prairie as if it wanted to dive under the dark, colorless, and unruly tangle of chaotic clouds beneath the coming storm.

Now the wind came in gusts behind him. Blanche could scarcely maintain his footing. Out of the turmoil in the northwest, a low wall of clouds emerged. It looked like one of Aunt Shoe Peg's rolling pins. It was barreling toward him, seemingly along the ground, and dirty gray. Bolts of lightning danced across the sky and illuminated patches of oblivion behind. The wall of cloud drove a blast of dust and dirt before it. Blanche's path led him straight into the storm, but he had no escape. The storm stretched across the sky.

The rolling cloud was within a hundred yards of Blanche when he was hit by a blast of air from the north. It was cold and full of dust and bits of debris that stung his flesh and pushed him backward to the ground. Now the rage of the prairie storm was on him and with it a torrential wall of rain. It fell in huge drops at first and then in sheets. In a moment, the runaway was drenched, soaked to the bone by rain that was colder than a well digger's fanny.

Behind the rain came a heavy shower of hail. Blanche had no shelter, no place to hide. He sat on the ground and hid his face between his knees. He covered his head with his forearms. Ice pellets the size of dimes pelted the prairie and stung his flesh. He was too busy covering himself to be afraid. A shaft of lightning blasted the ground not a hundred feet away. Thunder ripped the air with the sound of a tree splitting apart. In the bright flash of light, the hailstones around Blanche glimmered as if the prairie was covered with a blanket of diamonds.

The hail quit as quickly as it had started, and the rainfall returned. It was so heavy, he couldn't see his hand in front of his face. Suddenly it came down lightly, then not at all. A great hush overcame the glistening ground, and the prairie was swallowed in silence for the first time that day. Mist hung in the air like a shroud. It was as if the rain had taken a holiday with its ally, the wind, and stolen the cheery voices of the meadowlarks.

The turkeyfoot, some beaten back by the hail, saw a chance and tried again to reach the sky. Overhead, the clouds overhead churned in a boiling confusion with a sickly greenish hue.

In the space of minutes, a soaking rain returned. Once again Blanche was drenched and cold. He had nowhere to shelter himself. The water streaming down his face might have been tears, he didn't know. He felt like a drowned rat.

In an hour, the sun peeked out below the clouds for just long enough to say good night. It sank below the western horizon without offering warmth to the runaway who had cursed it earlier that day.

Back to the east, the tops of great pillowy clouds caught the last rays of the sun. Lightning frolicked across the belly of the storm and into the darkness below. Above him, the sky was clear. The hailstones had disappeared into the prairie earth.

Blanche laid his head on a wet prairie-grass bed. He was chilled, and his teeth chattered. His neck bowed; his eyes drooped with exhaustion. He sang to himself to ease his fears.

> *When the sun comes back and the first quail calls*
> *Follow the Drinking Gourd*
> *For the old man is waiting*
> *For to carry you to freedom*
> *If you follow the Drinking Gourd.*

He found comfort in the song for a reason he couldn't put his finger on. As the sky darkened and nighttime fell, ahead of him, in the north, the drinking gourd emerged, shimmering in the cold night sky. Then a mosquito tried to feast on his cheek, and he slapped it away.

The sting helped him forget his nerves. The storm had shaken him, scared the bejesus out of him, just like the hell's fire and the brimstone Methodist preacher of his dream.

Henry used to say, "Nothing but a bunch of wild-eyed holy rollers, those Methodists." Hard-bench Presbyterians like Henry couldn't bear to compliment the Methodists, and the Methodists made themselves an easy target for Henry's verbal barbs. They were always trying to bring the Indians to salvation. "Good God," Henry would say, "flopping and rolling around on the ground, I should say. We'd have savages quartered in every town in Missouri if that stupid ignorant filthy dirty Ohio mulatto had his way." Every time he talked about the mixed-race leader of the Methodists in the west, Henry seemed to exaggerate the insulting words even more than the last time he told it. He took to saying it in sing-song fashion: "O-HI-o mu-LATT-o." And if his cigar-chomping buddies didn't laugh hard enough, no worry—Henry laughed enough for everyone.

To Henry, all the Methodists were "stupid, ignorant, filthy, dirty." He rattled off that epithet all the time as if he didn't even have to think about what he was saying. Of course, Henry found a way to bite his tongue if he was selling a print job to the headmaster of that Shawnee mission school that was out on the prairie, four miles west of Westport. He was a preacher whose in-laws had been captured and raised by the Shawnees. The Missouri Methodists supported his school, and he always had a bale of religious literature to hand out. So at least a couple of times a month, Henry minded his words. For a few days, the Methodists weren't quite as stupid, ignorant, filthy, or dirty as Henry usually held them out to be. This might not have been so, but the evangelical Methodists outnumbered all the other denominations two to one, and they were eager to meet and help their brethren.

Blanche wished he had a bundle of those Methodist tracts to lay his head on. The prairie grass was wet and uncomfortable. In that fleeting moment that's not awake and not asleep, he wondered if the old man in the drinking gourd song was a Methodist.

11

— — —

The weary trail, the hunger and thirst, and the storm the night before had robbed all the bounce from Blanche's stride. The fevered flesh on his back ached from the beating it took from the hailstones and drove him forward. He came on a brushy line of tress, and his step didn't find a footing. He stumbled, spilling down a rock face, head over heels, and into a tiny stream. Coughing and sputtering, he struggled to regain his feet. The water was cold, but no more than waist deep. He sat back in the stream, and the cool water helped put out the fire on his back and shoulders.

He had difficulty dragging himself out of the water and back to dry land on the north bank. The little river had near-vertical limestone banks on both sides, and the roots of the prairie grasses above were higher than Blanche could reach. Only ropey tree roots offered to give the weakened and hungry runaway a handhold. Blanche felt like he was crawling up the side of a giant shoebox.

Eventually he slithered out on dry land, and lying in the grass, exhausted, he realized his ketchup bottle was gone. He cursed the river and promised himself to be more careful. Away to the north, Blanche could see a little village. It sat on the eastern side of a high bluff, perhaps two miles away. It might be Lawrence, and if the farm wife was right, that's where he would find a lamp that burned at noon.

Colonel Lane and his wife, Mary, followed the Oregon Trail when it broke off north from the Santa Fe Trail. On farther a ways, they paid a toll to a Frenchman and drove their rig on a bridge across a small boxy-bottomed stream, the Wakarusa River. Blanche would have seen the bridge, but he had shied away from the road, as the farm wife had warned him to do. North from the bridge a couple of miles, the colonel and his wife rode their buckboard off the prairie and into the little town of Lawrence, Kansas.

Ahead of them, the Lanes saw a little cabin with a picket fence. A burning lantern hung on the hitching post. "Look at that fool," Lane told his wife. "Burning his oil in broad daylight. I wish I had money to throw away."

Blanche stepped out of a wooded creek bed at the edge of town. He had been hiding across the road from a cabin with a burning lantern that hung from a gate in the yard. Near the cabin, a plain, rawboned young man turned the soil with a shovel. Blanche thought he looked like an overgrown farm boy.

"Get on the bald end of this shovel, boy."

Blanche looked around and realized the farm boy was yelling at him.

"Yes, Marse." Blanche scampered through a gate and into the yard surrounded by the picket fence. He took the shovel.

"Welcome, friends," the farmer hollered out again. This greeting was for the couple in the buckboard.

"Howdy. Is there lodging in town?" Lane asked the farmer.

Please tell them to keep moving, Blanche thought. The fewer pro-slavery people in town, the better he liked it.

"A fine boarding house, friend. On Massachusetts Street."

"You sound on the goose?" Lane asked.

The farm boy didn't hesitate. "Yessiree, I'm sound on the goose. Pro-slavery all the way." Blanche's heart sunk. *How could the prairie woman be so wrong? How could she send me straight to a slaveholder?*

Colonel Lane handed a sky-blue piece of paper to

the farmer. It had a list of names inside boxes and in the upper right-hand corner, a stylized symbol that looked like a rooster. Even from several feet away, Blanche could see that it was a ballot that he himself had printed. Henry had stamped the rooster symbol on a ballot that listed only Democrat candidates. That made casting a ballot easier for anyone who wanted to vote straight-party, who wanted all the offices filled by people of one party, especially illiterate voters.

Then the colonel burst into song.

> *Come on, all you roosters*
> *we all have to crow*
> *Because the Democrat Party*
> *has to grow.*

"Got a big election tomorrow!" Colonel Lane's voice carried like a ringing bell. "Us pro-slavery folks got us an obligation." Colonel Lane tossed a chaw of tobacco to the farm boy and then drove on.

Watching the buckboard trundle off toward town and out of earshot, the farm boy turned to Blanche and asked him pointedly, "Have you ever been on the railroad?"

The question took Blanche back to those minutes when he thought his mother had lost her sanity, when they dragged him from her side back in Virginia. He pictured her voicing this same question. He realized the farm boy was asking him a question in code. As his thoughts raced to recall a forgotten answer, he was flooded with remembrances of his mother. She wasn't crazy. He did know the answer. It was on his lips. He found the words spilling from his mouth. "I have been a short distance."

"Where did you start from?"

"The depot."

The farm boy's wife opened the door to her cabin, curious about the commotion outside. She held an infant in her arms.

The farm boy pressed on. "Where did you stop?"

And Blanche replied, "At a place called...safety."

"Come inside, friend," the farm boy's wife said. "Hurry."

The farm boy looked over each shoulder and then ushered Blanche inside the tiny one-room cabin. Before he himself entered, he muttered, "Election," as if it were a curse word. He threw the chaw of tobacco into the road.

Blanche ate like, well, a runaway slave. A toddler watched him across the table, his eyes as big as silver dollars. The wife pieced together a quilt—one with a wagon wheel pattern. The farm boy slid another plate full of food in front of Blanche. "Eat what you can, friend."

Looking at the quilt in the wife's lap, Blanche said, "The name's Blanche. Blanche Bruce...The wagon wheel. I know that sign."

The farm boy offered, "Sam Wood. And this is my missus, Margaret. My son, David, is the one who's watching you like a hawk."

Margaret reached across and felt of the fabric of Blanche's shirt. "These clothes are a disgrace," she said.

Wood pulled back Blanche's collar and saw a lash mark, still angry and fevered from Thomason's beating. A nauseating rage grew in Wood's belly. Often, when anger overtook him, he sang quietly, his voice softer than a baby's whisper. He sang a Quaker hymn, "How Can I Keep from Singing?"

No storm can shake my inmost calm
While to that refuge clinging
Since Christ is Lord of heaven and earth
How can I keep from singing?

Young David scurried from his seat and hid behind his mother's dress. His father's song gave him a fright. "Mama," he cried. "Daddy's gonna kill a man!"

"Mr. Wood," she scolded. "You scare the child."

Wood took a deep breath. "Maybe the newspaper's in."

Blanche brightened. "I'm a newspaper man. What day is it?"

Wood caressed David and the infant and then squeezed Margaret's hand. "March 29th. Eighteen fifty-five," Wood told him. "There's a lot of bushwhackers about, so you better not plan on heading out for another couple of days." He stuffed a pistol under his belt on the way out of the cabin. Wood's pistol was like some of the newer types Blanche had seen around Westport. They had a sort of a cylinder affair that clicked forward every time it was shot, and that gave the shooter five or six shots before having to reload. Five or six, that is, not counting the misfires. When the hammer dropped, it hit a tiny percussion cap that ignited a black powder charge packed inside the gun barrel. The system was faster than the old flintlocks but not as reliable. The caps didn't always fire, and when they did, they didn't always ignite the charge in the barrel. Single-shot pistols and rifles, even these new revolvers, all of them took forever to load, all except for this new rifle he'd been hearing talk about, the Sharp's rifle. Compared to the Kentucky squirrel rifles most Westerners used, the Sharp's rifle looked like a cannon. Unlike the muzzle-loaders, it was loaded from the breach, the end of the barrel closest to the shooter. It hinged open in the middle, and a mechanical assembly allowed the rifleman to insert a linen or paper cartridge into the barrel and then close the breechblock again. Like the muzzle-loaders, the shooter placed a percussion cap where the hammer fell so that when he pulled the trigger, the cap ignited the cartridge.

The Sharp's rifle could only fire a single shot, but the shooter could reload and fire nine times per minute. On his best day, the most skilled riflemen could only get off three shots a minute with a muzzle-loader.

Another feature of the Sharp's rifle that made it grist for the gossip mill was its range. The rifle was effective at five hundred to seven hundred yards. This range gave "Sharpshooters" another huge advantage over their opponents. With speed of reload and long range, an attacker might have to lose ten men in his quest to kill only one man armed with a Sharp's rifle. Those numbers could be even worse for an attacking force if the defenders were dug in.

Blanche had often listened in on boisterous debates in the print shop, those evening time discussions after the sun went down and the cigars came out. "A man can shoot the stripes off a skunk at five hundred yards with a Sharp's rifle," according to Henry, "and Lawrence has a skunk infestation."

A loud-mouthed Blue Lodger added, "Only a neighbor with hostile intentions would arm himself with a Sharp's rifle," and all of the others agreed.

Blanche stopped privately musing about guns when he realized Margaret was speaking to him.

"A fight's brewing," she said. "Mr. Wood thinks he can hide his hatred behind a song. The child knows. Blessed are the peacemakers."

"Beautiful words," Blanche said. "But sometimes you can't hardly make a peace."

"We're Friends. Quakers."

"Methodist. I guess. I had a master that was." Blanche returned to packing it in, but not before he noticed a Sharp's rifle lay like a baby in a crib in a gun rack over the fireplace.

12

— — —

The next morning, Wood tossed an axe in the bed of his buckboard wagon. "Come on friend," he told Blanche, "I'll give you a lay of the land, and we can fetch in a load of firewood." They headed north through the commercial district of Lawrence.

On Massachusetts Street, the main road through Lawrence, Blanche saw the storefront of a little shop with a big sign that said, *NEW ENGLAND EMIGRANT AID SOCIETY—TOWN LOTS, IMPROVED CLAIMS, REAL ESTATE FOR SALE*. That squared with things he had read in the Yankee papers. Abolitionists in Massachusetts were moving hundreds of northeastern families to Lawrence. To get their grubstake, all they had to do was move and promise to support free state causes.

The footing of a huge stone building was emerging from the ground at the north end of Massachusetts Street. It was crawling with stonemasons. The way they had it staked out, it looked to Blanche like the building was going to be a block long.

"What's going up there?" Blanche asked. "A fort?"

"A hotel."

"Mercy. You know, Mr. Wood, this is a pretty town. Growing fast. A lot of opportunity here, I reckon."

"It's nice until election day rolls around. Then the place fills up with Missouri pukes."

As a slave—former slave, Blanche thought happily—he was sure he could never get away from Missouri pukes. If they only came around on election day, he figured he could tolerate them. "I might just settle down here. I can run a press, you know that?"

"Be back in a minute." Wood tied the team to a post and entered the general store. Blanche stood down from the wagon to stretch his legs one more time before heading off to the country. A heated political argument was taking place at the front of a blacksmith's shop next door. It caught his attention. A peppery little redhead had his finger in the face of a couple of fellows with white ribbons tied through buttonholes in their lapels.

"The timber is on my land, and you keep off," the redhead said.

White men, arguing about property, Blanche thought. *Maybe things aren't so different in Kansas.*

A man leading a team and wagon stopped to listen. His wagon bed held several boxes of the blue ballots Blanche had printed back in Westport. He tied his team and stepped in, drawn to the fray like a bee to honey.

"The survey ain't done," the teamster chimed in. He spoke in a thick Irish brogue.

The quarrel amused Blanche, but his eye fixed on the unguarded boxes of ballots. No one was watching him. The bickering distracted the onlookers. He picked up a box of ballots from the Irishman's rig and put it in Wood's wagon.

The redhead ranted even though he was outnumbered. "Look, fool..."

One of the white-ribboned men shoved the Irishman aside to get back into the argument. "We run abolitionists off. We'll do the same with you."

"I ain't afraid of a bunch of chicken thieves," the redhead said. His complexion was florid. Painful burns flecked his skin. Cooking greenhorn rocks to make lime was work for slaves in Missouri. Hot caustic salts always splattered the men who tended a kiln. But the limekiln was making more money for the redhead in a week than he could make in a year back east. Since timber was in such short supply on the prairie, the kiln owner was hopping mad. The sinew stood out on his neck, as he stuck out his chin. He was dead set that his convictions were right. "I got a lime kiln to tend to, and I need that timber. So just quit cutting."

A crowd began to gather around the blacksmith shop, and Blanche moved another box of ballots into Wood's wagon. The Irishman was ready to scrap. "Why don't we step out back and settle this."

"You keep your fat mick nose out of my business," the redhead answered.

"You redheaded runt. I'll say what I like. It's a free country."

Blanche slid two more boxes of ballots into Wood's wagon.

"I hear you said you'd shoot me and that I'm abolition and gonna steal your slaves."

The Irishman had kept his powder dry longer than anyone would have imagined. "Get on back to your lime kiln, hothead."

The redhead paid the blacksmith—he had repaired a wagon tongue, called a singletree. It was long and awkward, but the redhead picked up one end and dragged it toward the prairie.

One of his rivals spat a black stream of tobacco juice onto the roadway behind him. "Jayhawkers."

"He said one more thing," the Irishman said, "I would have took him out back and thrashed him."

"I'd pinch his no good little red head off," the other said. "I had that redheaded dog in my sights once, and I ain't gonna pass up a chance like that again."

The blacksmith grabbed both of the men by their arms and squeezed. His grip must have bit like a vise. Each of them winced and stood on tiptoes.

"Okay. Enough of that. I won't have cheap talk in the shop," the blacksmith scolded. "If you can't behave civil, get out."

Blanche had moved seven boxes of ballots into the wagon when Wood exited the general store with a jug of whiskey.

Wood and Blanche rode over a ford in the broad river north of Lawrence.

"Is there anything in those boxes I need to know about?" Wood asked.

"A few extra ballots they won't be needing."

"Push them off in the river," Wood said.

"I thought you Quakers was peace lovers," Blanche said, watching the boxes float downriver.

"There's a fight brewing, and I've got every intention of being right in the middle of it. A man has responsibilities."

The whiskey jug jostled against the axe each time

a wagon wheel rolled over a stone in the rocky river bottom.

"And I also thought you Quakers were teetotalers."

"What's this?" Wood said, ignoring Blanche. On the far shore, a pair of horsemen and a buckboard wagon with two occupants awaited.

"Wolves!" Blanche said. It was Jones, Atchison, Thomason, and Stringfellow.

"Git yourself in the back and turn your face. Don't get far from that axe," Wood told the runaway. To tame his wrath, Wood sang under his breath. Sometimes it wasn't in vain.

Wood's team pulled his wagon out of the river as the foursome reached the ford. Blanche hunkered in the back. Stringfellow spilled out of his buckboard and onto the ground. On his hands and knees, he vomited. It was still early in the day, and he was stinking drunk.

"Hey, sodbuster," Jones said to Wood. "Don't tell me you voted already. You sound on the goose?"

Wood was calm. "Who am I talking to?"

"Samuel Jones. I'm the postmaster, Westport, Missouri." Jones slapped at a stray cigar ash on his vest.

"Samuel Wood. Yeah. I'm sound on the goose," Wood answered. He pretended to be pro-slavery so he wouldn't have to explain why an abolitionist was fording the river with a slave boy. Then pointing at Stringfellow, Wood asked, "Who's he?"

"He's Dr. Stringfellow. Runs the newspaper *Squatter Sovereign*."

"You Blue Lodge?" Stringfellow, recovering from his distress, sat back against the wheel of his buckboard and wiped his chin on his coat sleeve. "Let's see the sign."

Wood defiantly pulled the whiskey jug from the wagon bed and with a twist popped out its corncob stopper. After a big sip, he handed the jug to Thomason. "See if that don't chime the password," Wood said. "Why, you're that Senator. Atchison. Come all this way to vote?"

Atchison handed Wood a blue ballot with the rooster symbol. "Itching to exercise the franchise. Uh-huh-ahem. Jonesey here heard the, harrumph, clarion call to service, and he is gonna get himself elected your next sheriff."

Atchison chattered away. He seemed much more interested in the contents of the jug that he and his pals were passing around than the election. "Thought we might collar us a slave or two while we was at it. Kill two birds you might say."

Thomason added, "Yeah."

"You ain't seen or heard nothing about a fugitive

slave, I don't imagine?" Atchison flashed a boozy, jaundiced grin.

"Nary a word."

"A girl named Blanche?" A sick grin was smeared across Thomason's face.

"I don't reckon you got a flyer? Who's offering the reward? How much?"

"I don't got a flyer, Sam Wood," Jones said. "It's a maybe thing we just heard talk of."

"Yeah," Thomason added, "we don't need you cutting in our action."

"Nice to make your acquaintance, Senator, Postmaster. But me and my boy hear the clarion call of the timber. Ain't cutting itself, is it Moses?"

Blanche answered, "No sir, Marse Wood." Wood folded the blue ballot and carefully put it in a shirt pocket. While the slavecatchers passed the jug among themselves, the conductor's wagon pressed past them, on a road through the wooded riverbank, up and out of the bottom land, and toward the tall-grass prairie.

After noon, Wood and Blanche rode the wagon back into town loaded with firewood. They drove past a hack that was being tied to a hitch by a man dressed in black. In the bed of the wagon was the dead body of a redheaded man, his face obliterated by a smear of gore.

Wood asked the man, "What happened to him?"

"Lead poisoning. Shotgun, I reckon," the undertaker answered.

They found that a rabble of white-ribboned, jug-carrying, gun-toting ruffians had taken over Lawrence. The whiskey-soaked election had turned into a free-for-all that would put any Halloween revelry to shame.

The thugs surrounded the general store where Jones straddled the threshold like a colossus. Musket fire erupted, and the ruffians whooped. Sprinkled along Massachusetts Street, townsmen glared at the spectacle, speechless, powerless to act.

"This is where I vote. Follow me. I can't leave you here on the street alone," Wood said. He elbowed his way inside the general store, and with some unease, Blanche followed. Wood gave Blanche a penny and told him to buy a peppermint stick.

A Frenchman sat at a table behind a sign that identified him as "registrar." Hooligans swarmed him, eager to cast their blue ballots. Beyond him, a ladder led to the rafters. Up in the loft above the store, a poll watcher guarded a ballot box that was perched on a barrel. The election officials had anticipated a rowdy crush of voters—everyone would be able to figure out who his neighbor was voting for from the color of the ballot he cast anyway—but no one had ever figured out how to stop the voters from fighting and threatening one another at the poll. All they could do to keep peace near the ballot box was to station it at the top of a ladder so that only one voter at a time could approach.

Thomason loitered inside the store with Jones, Atchison, a tipsy Stringfellow, and as many ruffians as the store could hold. They were all armed to the teeth—their pistols and Bowie knives were on display.

Jones had a large stack of blue ballots. "Thomason, get over here," he said, handing Thomason a ballot. Jones jerked his thumb in the direction of the Frenchman with the register book.

"You a Kansas resident, sir?" the Frenchman asked.

Thomason turned to Jones. "What am I supposed to say?"

"You must be a resident to vote," the registrar said.

"Thomason, get your sorry carcass out of the way," Jones told the big bully, and Thomason stepped aside. Jones shoved his way through the crowd to the registrar's desk with a sick smile.

"Are you a resident of Kansas?"

"I am." Jones winked at the gang surrounding the registrar.

"Does your family live in Kansas?"

"None of your business," Jones answered. "Now keep your impertinence to yourself or I'll knock that fat head off your shoulders." He pulled a pocket-watch out of his waistcoat and opened it. "You got five minutes. Resign or you're a dead man."

The registrar tripped backward in a hasty retreat out the back door of the store. Jones grabbed the register book, an armful of blue ballots, and scrambled up the ladder and into the rafters, pistol drawn. The poll watcher didn't wait for orders. He dropped out of the loft and hooked a hot retreat out the back door as well.

"The people of Kansas got judges," Jones roared. "So does Missouri. Shucks, fair's fair." The candidate assumed the poll watcher's seat in the loft. He laid his pistol on top of the register book, and beside it, the stack of blue ballots.

Blanche looked through a window to see three tough characters chasing the registrar and the poll watcher, on foot, Bowie knives drawn.

Laughing and hiccoughing, Stringfellow climbed the ladder and picked a blue ballot from the top of Jones's pile. "John Stringfellow," he said.

Jones scribbled in the register book and read aloud, "John…Stringfellow. Got it. Someone fix that man a whiskey."

Stringfellow deposited his ballot and then descended the ladder. Atchison handed Stringfellow a bottle of whiskey, and he took a big slug.

Thomason bellowed, "Let me have a turn." He pulled a white-ribboned thug off the ladder and climbed into the rafters. He snatched away a blue ballot and stuffed it into the ballot box. "Horace Archlewis Thomason."

Jones wrote in the register book. "Horace… Archlewis…Archlewis? Whoa. Archlewis…Thomason," and Thomason climbed down the ladder with a grin.

Atchison yelled out to anyone that would listen, "Someone fetch a whiskey for the baby bull. Uh-huh-ahem."

Socking back a shot of rotgut, Thomason slobbered, "I could do this all day."

Jones's voice hollered down from the rafters, "Long as you can climb the ladder."

"A hundred dollars says I'll vote more than you," Stringfellow told Thomason.

"You're on." Thomason fought his way up the ladder again. "Horace Archlewis Thomason."

"Gimme a different name, jackass," Jones told him.

"Uh…John Stringfellow."

"He done voted."

"Make way," Stringfellow shouted. "I got names." Stringfellow pulled a book from his pocket. The cover read, *CITY DIRECTORY—A REGISTRY OF PROMINENT CITIZENS OF THE CITY OF SAINT LOUIS, MISSOURI.*

Blanche had kept out of the fray by hiding behind the counter of the general store. His peppermint stick didn't last long. He didn't have the patience to lick it down—he crunched it between his teeth. The voting made him nervous. He left the store by the back door and walked out a narrow alley between buildings. A bulletin board hung from the storefront near where the gang of thugs had tied their horses. He stepped across the road and onto the sidewalk to read the flyer.

> *RUNAWAY! Ran away from the subscriber in Westport, Missouri. To-wit: one dark mulatto, aged probably fourteen, stocky build, answers to the name BLANCHE, well dressed and bright.*
>
> *Reward of $250 will be paid for apprehension or $500 if taken beyond 100 miles of Westport and reasonable additional charges*

if delivered to the subscriber, the widow
A. Henry, at Westport. This fugitive has
for the past few years been the possession of
Edward H. Henry, Esq. of Westport.

Fear shot through his body like bolts of lightning. Thomason wouldn't be looking for a girl anymore. If he saw the flyer. If he could read. Blanche hid himself in an alleyway to wait for Wood.

A hullabaloo across the road ripped Blanche's attention back to the general store. A gauntlet of drunk ruffians was jostling Wood outside. The runaway was gripped with anger but too fearful to help his friend. Down the sidewalk, on Blanche's side of the road, Colonel Lane watched, his mouth wide open. The warrior that the paperboys would have followed to hell and back was standing aside, just watching.

Jones exited the store with the ballotbox under his arm. Blanche returned to his hiding place around the corner.

Thomason led the gang of ruffians that was trying to intimidate Wood. "Wasn't expecting anyone else to show up," he said, slurring his words. "We's plumb out of ballots, son. So the polls just closed."

"I brought my own," Wood told him. A long arm

reached out of the crowd, snatched away Wood's pale ballot and tore it to bug bites.

Stringfellow was totally snockered. "Come back tomorrow."

"Where's your ribbon?" Thomason roared.

"Let me pass. I come to vote, friend."

But Stringfellow insisted. "We voted plenty. Get a drink."

Jones wanted in on the fun. "Looky here. It's old Sam. My namesake. Sorry, Sam. No ballots left."

Colonel Lane finally took action. He swaggered across the roadway and pushed his way into the crowd of thugs who surrounded Wood. "Boys, ain't this putting it on a little thick?" Blanche wished he could stand up for Wood as Colonel Lane was doing now, but a black boy would have no influence over the Missourians.

All eyes were on Jones, who was now sullen. "You gone abolition?" The accusation was so combative that the rowdy mob fell silent.

Colonel Lane glared at Jones. Thomason stole Wood's pistol.

"Make way," Wood shouted. "I'm voting."

Thomason shoved Wood and yelled, "Watch your step." Wood tripped over an outstretched foot, and pro-slavery toadies mobbed him. One clubbed

Wood over the head with a short timber, and the farm boy hit the ground like felled tree.

"Hey," Thomason remembered, "I still got a hundred riding."

"Uh-huh-ahem." It was Atchison. "Still time for voting over to Eudora."

"It ain't enough to vote," Jones said. "You got to count 'em yourself if you want to win." Jones slung the stolen ballot box into Stringfellow's buckboard as his gang of thugs found their mounts.

"Hey, looky here," Thomason shouted. He had spotted the runaway poster on the bulletin board. "It ain't no girl. It's a boy." He ripped the flyer from the board, stuffed it in his pocket, and hoisted a big beefy leg up into his stirrup. His foot slipped out, and he spun around like a top. His ruffian pals laughed at the clumsiness of the drunken bully.

Thomason raised his fists to fight. "They better not be no one laugh," he shouted at the crew. "Cause I'm gonna find this here runaway slave and bring him in. And the hell with the rest of you. I'll show you who's the boss. You laughing jackasses, I'll show you."

The other ruffians muffled their chuckles and mounted horses and wagons, and the whole band rode for the edge of town.

No one came to the aid of Wood, lying unconscious in the roadway.

Colonel Jim Lane stood in the middle of the road, gaping at the gang of horsemen as they left Lawrence. He had been duped. Senator Douglas had promised him all the political patronage from Kansas Territory. All he had to do was stand down from his Congressional seat, bring in a Democratic majority in Kansas, and along with it, slavery. Then it was all his. He would be rich. He would be powerful. It had all been so simple.

Lane's career in politics had taught him that stealing an election was no way to nail down a permanent majority. Politics was politics, and sometimes it involved open warfare and bloodshed. But this kind of arrogant contempt for the law was short-sighted. He was willing to look the other way if a few Missouri boys voted in Kansas, but these whiskey-crazed fools had stuffed the ballot box like a Christmas turkey. The clowns were going to register twice as many votes in the election as there were men, women and children in Kansas Territory. Wait until *The New York Times* found that out. The election was going to prove what the Yankees had been saying all along. And it could only alienate the Westerners who usually didn't give a tinker's cuss about slavery one way or the other. Any Indiana man worth his salt would die fighting on a hill before he would let someone cram an election down his throat.

All his plans, shot in the head for one stupid election. All his prospects, ruined. Atchison and all his potential political support was riding out of town, having turned their backs on Colonel Jim Lane. The patronage Douglas pledged was running through his fingers like water. All his dreams, dashed on the rocks. Waves of self-doubt washed over and swallowed up Colonel Lane.

He watched now as the townsmen of Lawrence dispersed. Blanche came out of hiding. No one but the runaway was on hand to witness Colonel Lane lose contact with reality.

He faced the south wind and shouted. "Come back here, you! I won't stand for this! I'm going to take this fight to the Governor! I'll hunt you down, every last one! You better run, you cowards!"

Colonel Lane stumbled to the side of the roadway and sat on a sidewalk with his feet in the street. He drew his pistol and rested it in his lap. He was grief-stricken, anguished, and terrified—scared to death he'd never again lead men into a fiery combat. He would be ordinary. It was a thought too frightening to consider. His body trembled. Tears swelled in his eyes. He looked down the barrel of his pistol and ran his finger along the trigger.

Blanche had seen enough blood for one day. He

ran to Colonel Lane's side and seized the pistol. He threw it as far as he could.

The fugitive thought he should see to Wood's well-being, but the madness that had overtaken the grim warrior on the sidewalk unsettled him. "You need to go help that man." Blanche snapped to get Lane's gaze to turn and focus on Wood. "He's a fighter. You need him."

Lane got to his feet and staggered toward Wood. His step looked to Blanche to be getting firmer as he neared Wood.

Now frightened for his own skin, Blanche ran to Wood's wagon, grabbed the axe and a gunnysack, and took off on foot, north. *Someone else can patch the Quaker farm boy up. I'm not his keeper,* Blanche thought, hating himself for allowing the thought to cross his mind.

He ran, past the man in black who carried the dead body of the redhead over his shoulder. A macabre longshoreman. Blanche didn't look back. He fought his way across the ice-cold river north of town with one thought in mind, to put as much prairie between himself and Lawrence as he possibly could.

13

— — —

The only sound Blanche heard was that of the wind and the scratchy murmur of the brittle turkeyfoot spikes banging against one another. He opened one eye and then the other. It was morning, and he was cold and wet from dew. A ladybug climbed a blade of grass not an inch from his nose. He stood to survey the countryside to his north.

The prairie was becoming more rolling. Little hillocks popped up more frequently now. Here and there the hillsides were broken with rock outcroppings that looked like dormers on a roofline, or slits of a cat's eye. Long and low, they exposed three or four feet of the capstone rock layer near the top of the knolls.

The fugitive wished he'd had time to draw out some information about the next stop on the Underground Railroad from the Quaker. He'd gone into Lawrence looking for a lantern that burned at noon—not much to go on, but something was better than nothing. Now the drinking gourd in the night sky was his only sign, his only friend.

Ahead, to the north and west, a herd of buffalo grazed.

Blanche had no interest in seeing the herd up close. He'd seen wagon after wagon rolling through Westport loaded down to the springs with shaggy buffalo skins, and the great beasts had a reputation for being ill-tempered. He decided to steer clear and adjust his heading to bear a bit more toward the northeast. *Better safe than sorry.*

As morning wore on, he skirted the eastern edge of a low bluff. He thought he heard thunder from the west, but the sky was cloudless. As he walked across the top of a rock outcrop, without warning he felt something latch onto his ankle and then he was falling off the ledge and onto the gravel below.

An Indian was lying beside him. The low rumbling sound was louder now, and Blanche struggled to find his feet. He was startled by the tumble from the ledge, and even though he was angry, he knew he needed to be upright if he were to mount any defense against the Indian. He guessed the brave must be six and a half feet tall. He decided he had better run. When he tried to pull away, the Indian shoved the muzzle of a rifle under his jaw.

"Let me go!" he yelled, but his voice was drowned out by the thundering noise.

The Indian gestured to Blanche with a long index finger. He made a slashing gesture across his throat. Blanche decided it was best to pipe down. The rumbling had become deafening. It sounded as if a freight train were passing by a foot from his ear.

Off to the left and right, beyond the ends of the rock ledge, before the sky went dark, Blanche saw Indian braves riding bareback.

The sky filled with buffalo hooves and under-bellies. The Indians had stampeded them toward the rock ledge, and the shaggy beasts had to jump from the waist-high ledge to the gravel flat below. Blanche and the Indian lay as flat against the rock face as they could and kept their heads as low as possible to avoid the flying hooves.

A cow stumbled after jumping from the top of the outcrop. As she slowly tried to regain her legs, the Indian with Blanche fired his musket. The cow crippled again. She regained her footing but was only able to trot a short distance.

Now the Indian braves who had driven the herd over the bank returned to swarm the injured cow with arrows and spears. Blanche had supposed that a hundred braves must have stampeded the herd, but the final kill was carried out by no more than a dozen hunters. His eyes searched for an escape, but his captor prodded him toward the kill with the business end of his musket. It no longer carried a charge, but it was wielded by one big Indian. And he carried a Bowie knife inside his knee-length laced moccasin. He took Blanche's axe and gave it to one of the braves. He put it to good use on the heavy joints of the buffalo.

"Let me go, will you? I'm not going to do you any harm. White men pursue me," Blanche said. "Wolves!" to emphasize his meaning.

"This is the land of the people of the wind. Kanza. From the river west to the great mountains. I am a leader among them."

"I'm just passing through. And if you don't mind, I'll be on my way."

Before Blanche could make good on his words, he felt someone grab him from behind. The chief spoke. "You trespass. What price do you offer?" The Indian sat on his haunches while the others threw themselves into the task of gutting the buffalo cow.

"I can give you my axe." The butchering had gone so far now that the Indians had opened the abdomen of the cow and were feasting on her raw internal organs.

"You offer me an axe that belongs to my third wife's brother?"

"I have money. Twenty dollars. Forty dollars."

The chieftain was silent.

"Speak your name to my real wife's brother," the big Indian told him, "before he kills you." Blanche considered again making his escape but then imagined the feeling of the cold steel of a Bowie knife at his throat.

"Blanche."

All the Indians laughed, except for their leader. One of the hunting party had handed him a piece of liver, and he sat on the ground. He bit into the liver, cut off a piece with his Bowie knife, and began chewing. "Blanche. The braves are amused that you are a white black man," he said. The hunters obviously understood some French, that *Blanche* meant "white." "My name is Allegawaho."

One of the braves spoke to the leader in a scolding, guttural tone that Blanche was sure meant "kill him." Blanche struggled against the grip of the strong Indian brave.

"White. With hair of buffalo." He took another bite of the liver. "The blood of white buffalo on hands of Kanza. Bad medicine," he said. Standing, he rendered his verdict to the hunting party in English. "We will not kill the black white man. Maybe, one day, the Pawnee will kill him. But not us."

Allegawaho offered some of the raw liver to

Blanche, and he couldn't have been more gracious with his rejection.

"You come from Missouri?"

"Missouri. Yes. Missouri."

"Methodist?"

"Absolutely. Yes."

Allegawaho's nod told the runaway that the big hunter considered himself a Methodist too.

By the time Allegawaho had reloaded his old muzzle-loader, the hunting party had finished disjointing the cow.

Most of the Indians were lifting and cinching the heavy cuts of meat onto the backs of their ponies, but one was eyeing Blanche suspiciously. His hands tugged and stretched at a handful of the cordage the others were using to tie down their prize. Blanche didn't want to be bound, so he jumped to the side of a brave who was struggling to help boost a haunch of the cow over the back of his skittish horse.

Without a word, Allegawaho led his band off across the prairie. Blanche hung back, as if he thought the Indians might forget about him, but Allegawaho motioned for him to follow with the muzzle of his musket.

As the sun neared the horizon, the hunting party trudged into a creek bottom where patches of land were cultivated. A few women and children were tending a spring garden with primitive hoes, rakes, and digging sticks. Blanche recognized their crops: corn, beans, and squash.

Upon seeing the returning hunters, the women and children let out joyous yelps and ran to follow the men.

Soon they entered a village of three lodge houses. They were roughly circular, framed in wood and covered with earth. In places, Blanche could see that mats of woven grass and bark were under the earthen covering. The largest of the three must have been sixty feet across.

The happy shouts from the gardeners were soon joined by shouted greetings from the villagers and barking dogs. Blanche noticed that some of the villager's clothes were leather, and he assumed that they were homemade, while some looked like they came off the rack at Izzy's Cut-Price Dry Goods store.

Allegawaho was even taller that Blanche had first guessed, and Blanche quickly assessed that his status in the community was quite high. All the braves obeyed his guttural commands. The few young boys in the camp followed him like puppy dogs. As nightfall approached, he directed Blanche with a gesture to seat himself on a log beside a central campfire. An old and snaggle-toothed woman handed him a bowl of buffalo, boiled tender, with nuts and berries. He devoured it hungrily.

As evening wore on, Allegawaho and the hunting party came to sit beside the campfire. They groaned in protest for having to move and rubbed their bellies as if they'd eaten enough for a lifetime. The women and children gathered outside the inner ring and giggled when one of the men groaned in pretended torture as he threw a dried buffalo patty on the fire.

One of the older men lit a cigar with a twig from the campfire. After a puff or two, he said a few words and passed it on. The men passed the cigar to one another, each saying a few words in the Kanza language. Blanche was unable to understand what they said, but he got the drift. They were rehashing the details of the successful hunt, bragging and exaggerating the role each individual hunter played in the hunt that had filled their empty bellies. Allegawaho puffed the smoke and watched it drift away on the wind into the night sky. He handed the cigar to Blanche.

The silence was deafening. Blanche was as jumpy as a cut cat. So he talked. "Back on the Blue Ridge, the old folks tell about when Wolf cornered old Bobtail. Bobtail says, 'Wolf, you're strong and swift. But there's a creature whose powers have no match.' Wolf says, 'You'll both fill my belly. Let him show his face.' Bobtail stoops down and uncovers his friend, a tar baby. And Bobtail says, 'Go get him, Piskey!' Now the Wolf leaps on Piskey. He slaps Piskey with both front paws. They stick fast. He claws out with hind legs that stick to the Piskey too. Now Wolf bites the Piskey. Now he's stuck so tight he can't move. His mouth is so full of tar, he can't even growl."

Allegawaho said, "Yes. Good." The other braves murmured and nodded to one another in what seemed to be an acceptance. Blanche puffed on the cigar, coughed, and passed it on to an elder, a chieftain with piercing eyes.

After a puff or two, he spoke out in English. He looked directly at Blanche, as if the story had a special meaning for the runaway. "Sharp and cunning is the raccoon. The Kanza know him as Spotted Face. One evening a crawfish wandered along a river bank, looking for something dead to feast upon. A raccoon was also out looking for something to eat. He saw the crawfish and formed a plan to catch him. He lay on the bank and pretended to be dead. By and by the crawfish came near. 'Ho,' the crawfish thought, 'here is my feast. But is he really dead?' So he went near and pinched the raccoon on the nose and then on his soft paws. The raccoon never moved. The crawfish then pinched him on the ribs and tickled him so that the raccoon could hardly keep from laughing. The crawfish at last left him. 'The raccoon is surely dead,' he thought. And he hurried back to the crawfish village and told the chief of his great find. All the villagers were called to go down to the feast. The chief told the warriors and young men to paint their faces and dress for a dance. So they marched in a long line. First the warriors, with their weapons in hand and then the women with their babies and children. To the place where the raccoon lay. They formed a great circle about him and danced and sang. 'We shall have a great feast on the spotted-faced beast, with soft, smooth paws. He is dead! He is dead! We shall dance! We shall have a good time. We shall feast on his flesh.' But as they danced, the raccoon suddenly sprang to his feet. 'Who is that you say you are going to eat? He has a spotted face, has he? He has soft, smooth paws, has he? I'll break your ugly backs. I'll break your rough bones. I'll crunch your ugly, rough paws.' And he rushed among the crawfish, killing them by scores. The crawfish warriors fought bravely and the women ran screaming, all to no purpose. They did not feast on the raccoon. The raccoon feasted on them!"

Blanche enjoyed hearing the story but he didn't know what it meant. He wondered if he could escape the Kanza if he played dead. *Not likely,* he thought.

The cigar completed its circuit around the camp-fire, and again it was Blanche's turn. He puffed on it, coughed, and as he passed it on, he told Allegawaho, "Listen, I do appreciate the food. Maybe I ought to be on my way tomorrow."

"Here you are safe from the wolves."

"I know that."

"I've taken many prisoners."

"I'll be safer when I get north."

"You lived with white men?"

"Yes. Well, no."

"Cherokee? Choctaw?"

"What you asking?"

The elder spoke to Allegawaho in their native tongue.

"How much you worth as ransom?"

"Not much, I reckon. Twenty dollars. Give or take."

Allegawaho exchanged more words with the chieftain and then said, "You understand them... trading with them...understand what they say and what they think..."

"Perhaps."

"My third wife has a sister who cries in the lodge for a husband."

Blanche didn't catch on, even as the snaggle-toothed Indian woman returned to the campfire to collect utensils.

"She keeps a good fire. Like my real wife."

The snaggle-toothed woman smiled broadly at Blanche, and he started to see the outline of a picture that Allegawaho was drawing out.

"I haven't been with a woman."

"Older woman. Good way to learn."

"Let me…uh…" Blanche's mind raced to find a way to explain his position to the chieftain. They might both be Methodists, but Allegawaho was offering this woman to him like he was offering a slice of sweet potato pie.

"You'd have a high place. My kinsman. An able wife." The Indian was finished with his offer. It was gracious to offer but not gracious to insist.

"I'll think on it a spell," Blanche said. He hid his face in an empty bowl, pretending to gorge on food. The chieftain might be right. A life with the Indians held some attractions.

With the exception of a few kisses he had stolen from Sis, he had no experience with the opposite sex. He did want to find a woman, someday, someone to share a life with. Someone who could cook cornbread and beans with a little fatback. And collards. And buttermilk and fried chicken. His poor stomach was so gorged with buffalo right now that he thought it would split wide open, yet he was thinking about the kind of food he'd never get to eat in an Indian camp. He'd have to get used to buffalo, dried buffalo, and nuts and berries, and little shelter from the winter cold.

Allegawaho offered a place to hide from slave-catchers, if any were to come after him. Maybe. He doubted that any of the Indians owned a book or could read. That was enough to nix the deal.

When he looked up, Allegawaho and the Indian braves and elders were gone. One by one, the women and children drifted away to other campfires. All but the snaggle-toothed Indian woman, the chieftain's third wife's sister. She smiled at Blanche.

It was the next morning and Blanche was taking his leave from the Indian village. During his stay in their camp, he had lost his fear of them. "You don't want my third wife's sister," Allegawaho said. "So be it. You could stay here and be my slave."

"Slave? You don't plant cotton. Or tobacco. Or print newspapers."

"As a prisoner of Allegawaho, you will have a high place."

"You've been awfully kind to me."

"My third wife's sister will cry by the fire until you return to our flock of turkeys."

"If the wolves find me here, it will be worse for you."

"The wolves chase us too. To one stream, then another. Soon they will chase us over the far mountains."

"Thank you, friend."

Blanche was surprised when Allegawaho gave him back his axe. The warrior also gave him a small cherty rock. It was a node of flint, smaller than his palm. "My third wife's brother wants you to have his axe."

"Tell him thanks for me, would you?"

Blanche handed the warrior two twenty-dollar bank notes from his wallet, but the warrior shook his head.

"Gold. Paper no good."

Blanche returned the bank notes to his wallet and pulled out a twenty-dollar gold piece.

Allegawaho was satisfied. "Watch out for the Pawnee," he told the runaway.

Blanche woke the next morning with a start. He'd been lying in his prairie-grass bed, dreaming of the Indian elder with piercing eyes and the campfire story about the raccoon and crawfish. He was less sore today and not as cold. The night before, he'd been able to get a fire going by striking Allegawaho's flint on the back of his axe. It produced lots of hot, reliable sparks that he fired into a nest of dry grass.

He was, however, hungry as usual. He stretched to loosen the stiffness in his bones, tucked the flint in his pocket, and lifting his axe over his shoulder, headed out, north again, across the prairie.

From time to time now, he passed shrubby trees, not merely in the low ravines but on the slopes of the rolling hills. Often, their trunks were scarred with black. Blanche reasoned that the trees had somehow withstood a prairie fire, one accidentally set by lightning or purposefully set by Indians hoping to improve the range for buffalo.

He began to notice, too, that large boulders dotted the prairie, as if scattered there by giants. The incline of each hill seemed steeper. The muscles in his thighs burned each time he crested a hill.

At the end of the day, rather than being able to see the horizon from each rise, he was only able to see to the top of the next ridge, two or three miles ahead. The low troughs between the hills were now choked with trees, and Blanche was happy to find that these little valleys generally hid tiny creeks.

On toward sunset, on his second day after leaving Allegawaho's village, he decided to camp by a creek, the largest he'd come upon since the big river by

Lawrence. The banks of the stream were steep, and a snarl of woody vegetation tumbled twenty feet down to the bed of a tiny stream.

The water was disagreeably muddy, but Blanche drank enough to satisfy his thirst and then washed out his clothes. Across the creek, not ten feet away, several soft-shelled turtles soaked up the last of the day's warm sun. The turtles were fast, but Blanche was faster. He dove headfirst across the stream and snagged a turtle by a back leg.

With one stroke of this axe, off came the turtle's head. Blanche built a fire. It was easy to feed the flames with the dead wood that choked the creek bed. He roasted the turtle, still in its shell, by laying it on its back on the coals.

The meat was wet and sticky; the fat was snotty and reminded him of rolled oats that had been boiled too long. But soon, nothing was left of the turtle but the burned shell, bones, and innards. By the flickering firelight, Blanche impaled the innards on a stick and lured four crawdads to his feast.

The next morning, Blanche left his campsite by the creek, struggled up the woody tangle of brush on the north bank, and headed out, north again, up a rise to the next ridge with his axe and a pocketful of turtle guts.

The hills were higher now and the valleys more narrow. That next night, he camped on a riverbank. *A good place to build a town,* he thought. *Plenty of water here.* He would have eaten roasted crawdad tails until he popped wide open, but he ran out of turtle guts.

In the evening of the next day, from atop a hill, away in the distance to the east, he could see a dark-green plain covered by trees. The lush forest told him that his northward trek was now converging on the river, which he knew angled off in a north by north-westerly direction from Westport. He'd expected to run into the river sooner or later. He wondered about a band of green that seemed to stretch beyond the forest, north and south as far as the eye could see. This ribbon of green was tinged with a hazy, pale purple, as distant mountains looked in a picture book he'd seen in Virginia. He decided that the freedom side of the river had tall bluffs. It must be Iowa, and Iowa must look like Virginia.

14

— — —

Blanche continued trudging northward, up and down across the hilly country, still dragging the axe he'd nabbed in Lawrence. He had not seen a farmhouse in days. Hunger dogged every step. Since running out of turtle guts, his crawdad hunts had all come up empty-handed.

He was startled when a cottontail rabbit sprang from hiding just steps ahead of him. It ran lickety-split straight ahead—*north*, Blanche told himself, *smart rabbit*—but soon he saw that the rabbit began to circle back. Before Blanche had walked another hundred yards, the rabbit had returned to his original hiding place.

I wish I could run like a rabbit. I could cover some ground for sure. Live off grass, never go hungry. But then he thought about the rabbit circling back. *But that's one thing I will never do. Go back. I'll never go back. Not once I'm free. Never.* After listening to his stomach growl for another mile, he thought, *If I went back now, they'd beat me within an inch of my life. But at least I wouldn't starve to death.* But then, while thinking of a way to snare a rabbit, over the top of the tallgrass, Blanche saw a farmhouse and barn. He was feeling so desperate that he decided to take a closer look at the farm.

As he neared, Blanche crouched low behind the clumps of turkeyfoot grass and then came upon a boulder. Peering over the big stone, he saw a corral that held a prancing young horse. A blue tick coonhound bayed at the strange figure that watched the farm from behind the boulder, but lucky for Blanche, the hound eyed a cat and chased him away instead, around the corner of the barn.

A wagon wheel quilt hung from a window.

He crept to another rock that was within a hundred yards of the house, and he saw a man and a woman leave the place in a light wagon. When they were out of sight, Blanche circled to the back door. He heard only the voices of women.

He knocked and shouted, "Missus, could you kindly spare a traveler a bite to eat?"

Blanche was welcomed by two white girls about his age who served him generous portions of bread and milk.

"I sure do thank you, Missy. Both of you."

The one called Abigail said, "My daddy would whup us both good…"

"…if he thought we turned away one of God's creatures." The sister called Zelda finished Abigail's sentence. "Folks say Papa's…"

"…abolition," Abigail said.

"I could help out. I mean, if your father has work. I'm happy to pay him for the vittles."

"Will you stay?" Zelda asked. "Ma and Pa…and my brother—"

"Brother?" Abigail's face twisted.

Zelda continued. "My brother…Leonard…"

"…they're gone to the meadow to make hay." Abigail finished. Blanche hadn't seen a third person with the couple. It was just like when folks hung a "bad dog" sign when they didn't have a dog. Blanche didn't believe the girls had a brother at all.

Zelda propped her fists into her sides. "Abigail! He might be a fugitive."

"Are you a fugitive?"

Blanche thought about the wagon wheel quilt. Didn't that mean they were okay with fugitives? Maybe the parents had kept their work a secret from their daughters, or maybe this was just a protective move by the girls. Blanche pulled his wallet from his pocket. "No, Missy. I got my freepapers. I'm just headed north."

Zelda's lower lip rolled out. "I guess that's what you'd say…"

"Zelda? Look at his feet. They look…"

"…awful big."

"Could you use another pair of shoes?"

"Abigail?"

"Zelda, go upstairs. Get in Lee Roy's wardrobe. There's two or three pairs of boots that he's outgrown."

"Lee Roy? Don't you mean Leonard?"

"Come on. I'll show you." Abigail turned to Blanche. "If you do stay, I'm sure Father will be happy to put you out of reach."

"No, I can't stay."

"Come on, Zelda. Let's find those boots." *She doesn't need her sister to help her find a pair of old boots,* Blanche thought. *She's up to something.* Blanche stood at the foot of the narrow stair where he could overhear the sisters' conversation in the bedroom above.

Abigail was telling her sister, "I read it in town. He answers the description."

"He's going to have his animal way with us," Zelda said.

"Here's our chance. Don't you want to get off this old hard-scrabble rock farm?"

"The beast."

"Can you imagine what we can buy with two or three hundred?" Abigail's words danced.

Blanche was disappointed that the girls were scheming against him and more than a little vexed that they thought he was so stupid that he couldn't see through their shenanigans. Their footfalls on the creaky stair told him that the sisters were returning to the kitchen, so when Abigail appeared with a pair of worn-out boots, she found the runaway sitting in the chair by the kitchen table.

"Sister," Abigail said, "make sure you have the R-I-F-L-E. And make sure H-E doesn't L-E-A-V-E. I told Daddy I would go and see after the cows."

Zelda told Blanche, "We got chores to see after."

"So I'm leaving now to go see after the cows," Abigail added.

"Don't be long," Zelda yelled at her sister as she shot out the kitchen door.

Blanche finished off his bread and milk. Out a window he could see Abigail head off on foot. With a glance over her shoulder as though to assess if she was out of sight of the house enough, she started running and disappeared over a rise in the direction of the wagon tracks left by the man and woman on the wagon.

Blanche turned back to Zelda. She held a dirty

platter in front of her as if it were a shield. She backed away from Blanche, toward a rifle that stood in the corner.

Blanche leapt from the chair and grabbed Zelda by the wrist. "No you don't."

"Oh, woe," Zelda cried out, "he's going to have his beastly passion!"

"Quiet."

"He's going to take me in the flower of my youth!"

She must think I'm a stupid animal, Blanche thought. *The last thing I need is a tussle with a crazy woman bent on accusing me of taking advantage.* His only desire had been to get his belly full of food and then hit the trail again. He probably already had slavecatchers on his tail, and Zelda's notion of his beastly passion was the kind of thing that sold newspapers. It would be sure to put every farmer in the territory either on his trail or on the lookout. "I ain't gonna hurt you. Now would you please keep it quiet."

"You're not going to have your way? Go ahead, my eyes are sealed shut. Oh, the horror."

Blanche tied up Zelda at her wrists and ankles and stuffed a dish towel in her mouth. "If I wanted a woman, I'd be back at that Indian lodge, so just hush up."

He left the knots loose. He only wanted the restraints to hold long enough for him to put some distance between himself and the farm. *Poor kid, a dusty little prairie town must look like Saint Louis to her.* Then he raided the pantry. He found a joint of mutton, a loaf of bread, and a lump of butter. He dumped them all in a pillow case and was out the door with the worn-out boots and the rifle.

He fired the rifle down the well. No sense in letting Zelda use it against him. The well swallowed the sound of the rifle fire. The colt in the corral didn't even flick his ears. He threw the rifle aside. It was too heavy to carry and useless since it was unloaded. His axe was far more useful.

Zelda's voice squalled from inside the farmhouse and made Blanche wish he'd pulled on the knots harder. The sound of her voice told him that she'd been able to spit out her gag, and he feared that she was getting free of her bonds quicker than he'd intended.

Blanche crawled between rails and into a corral. He pulled on the boots. He stomped around in piles of horse manure, and as he did so, he took two or three mouthfuls of the mutton. The farmer's blue tick hound jumped on him and begged, eager for bite of the lamb.

Blanche bit off a morsel of mutton from the joint and tossed it to the hound. With a short piece of rope, he tied the rest of the meat to the colt's back leg.

Then he opened the gate to the corral and swatted the colt on the rump. The young horse kicked his heels and ran toward the gate and the open prairie beyond. The joint of mutton chased along behind the colt, bouncing up and down like a sick robin's butt, and after it the hound, in hot pursuit, barking up a storm. Blanche figured the colt would run until the hound stopped chasing him and that the farmer would be more worried about his livestock than one runaway. Blanche bent to grab up his axe. He heard the squeak of the gate. And then:

"What's your hurry, son?" It was the farmer, his wife, and Abigail. The farmer had closed the gate before the colt and the hound had broken free.

Blanche was trapped in the corral. He had no place to run. He looked the farmer in the eye and spoke with defiance. "Sorry, Marse, sir, but that squalling girl of yours gave me the jitters."

The farmer held his hand beside his mouth and yelled out, "We hear yah, Zelda. Now quieten down now, yah hear? Abigail, go tell your sister to shut it off." Zelda's screaming stopped. "She's a might flighty sometimes, I reckon."

Blanche wondered whether to trust the farmer. "She was mighty kind with me. Is there any work I can do to repay your generosity?"

The farmer took stock of Blanche. "Have you ever been on the railroad?"

A great rush of relief washed over Blanche. "I have been a short distance."

"Where did you start from?"

"The depot."

"Where did you stop?"

"At a place called safety."

"There's a rig coming this way out on the road. We don't have much time."

The farmer's hound sniffed at Blanche and wagged his tail. He scratched the hound's ears and smiled from ear to ear.

15

— — —

The farmer pushed aside a pile of hay and pulled open a wooden door in the dirt floor of the barn. A ladder extended down into a dark shaft. "Welcome to the Caldwell Fraidy Hole."

Blanche's flesh crawled. He was certain that the cavity was home to spiders, snakes, and all kinds of creepy-crawlies. The trapdoor closed behind, and once again, fear was his companion. Blanche could hear Caldwell tromping around over the door. Then a scraping sound that made the runaway imagine that the farmer was dragging a dead body over the entryway.

Particles of dust sifted through gaps in the door and spilled down the shaft and into the fusty fraidy hole. A single beam of sunlight shone through a pin-sized hole in the hatch. Dust, suspended in midair, flickered in the shaft of light but did nothing to illuminate the pitch black interior of the hideaway. It could have been only minutes before the hound began to sing out a warning. Soon, the sounds of a creaking wagon and the heavy breathing of horses cast themselves into the darkness of the fraidy hole.

"You mind it if we water my horses, sodbuster?" The voice Blanche heard belonged to Thomason.

Caldwell answered Thomason, but now he spoke with a hoosiery burr. "Hep yourself, traveler." He was acting dumb for Thomason just the way the slaves had to do when they talked to the slave drivers and patrollers.

"Mind if I look around?" Thomason's question sounded more like an order. *He must be inside the barn*, Blanche thought. *I can hear him clearer now.*

The hound was baying at the top of his lungs. "Git over here, Husband," the farmer's wife's voice told him, and the hound quit barking.

"That's his name? Husband?" Thomason asked. "How's the old man know if you're calling him or the dog?"

A woman's voice answered, high and crackly. "I wouldn't never talk to a dog like I talk to him."

"I say-o," Caldwell added.

"Well, I swan to goodness," Thomason said. "I never seen such a fine hound dog. Say, old feller, you sound on the goose?"

Blanche hoped that Caldwell knew the pro-slavery code words.

"Goose? HeeEEELL yeah. Me and Husband takes ours with biscuits and gravy. Good eating, I say-o."

Blanche winced.

"A biscuit-eating hound dog. I do declare."

"The old woman throwed me out the house one night, and I says, I says, 'Say-o, woman, would you throw a starving man a biscuit?' And sure as I'm standing here, say-o, she swabs a biscuit in a skillet full of bacon cracklings, kicks the door open, and wings that biscuit straight at my head. Darn sure did, she did. Heavy as a brick. That there pup jumped on it and snapped it down like a wolf, I say-o. I never even had a chance to get a sniff. Been eating biscuits ever since."

"He for sale?"

"I guess I better keep him. Say-o, the old woman sorta likes him."

"Tell you what," Thomason said. "I'll give you a silver dollar for that biscuit-eating hound dog. I been looking around for a good possum dog."

"Not my pup," the woman's voice said.

"Oh don't think he'd make much for a tracker. Less'n your possum had a biscuit tied around his neck, I say-o."

"You know anyone round these parts got tracking dogs?" Thomason's voice trailed off, and Blanche supposed the visitor had left the barn.

Blanche thought his breathing must sound like a steamboat on the river and was amazed that Thomason had not heard him. He thought back to how he could hear the wheezing of the Missouri River steamboats all the way to Westport. He was sure his heartbeat must be rattling the rafters in the barn above, even after Thomason was gone. The fear in this black hole didn't give him the energy that had coursed through his body when he took the strongbox from the widow's bedroom. His mind was racing. He gripped his knees close to his chest and sobbed, hoping he could choke back a scream if one sprouted in his belly.

His body shook as if he were cold, but sweat drenched his shirt. He remembered hearing folks say, "The Lord is my shepherd," and for a moment, he had faith that the Good Shepherd would put down his fear and he could bide his time in the fraidy hole in calm. Then he remembered the preacher, when they put the dead bodies of Reuben and Sally in the cold ground, raising up a terrible cry to the heavens about walking through the valley of the shadow of death. He began to tremble again. He imagined that the fraidy hole was a grave and that he was listening to what the preacher was saying over his own bones—about his spirit "going over Jordan."

Going over Jordan. Sometimes it means you're dead, and sometimes it means you're free.

His fear gave way to resentment. He wished a Bible-thumping preacher was squatted at his side right now in the cramped fraidy hole. *I want a straight opinion, preacher,* he'd tell him, *just to clear up the confusion once and for all. If I'm going over Jordan, like you say, am I dead? Or am I free? It can't be both things at the same time.*

And once you answer that, tell me what I'm supposed to think when I learned from the Bible that Moses killed an overseer, then somebody else comes along and tells the slaves to obey their masters.

He hoped it was someone other than Jesus who had said that last part, because more than ever, right now "obey your master" seemed like the most ridiculous thing he'd ever heard, and he didn't like going against Jesus. Maybe God was just making up his opinions to suit his pocketbook, like Henry.

Then he thought of Sis and wished he were sitting next to her under a tree by the creek, teaching her to read, and the trembling eased.

Once he could feel his breath come easier, Blanche crawled up the ladder and tried to push open the trapdoor. It wouldn't budge. *I can't stay here a minute longer!* He pushed again.

The trapdoor opened a crack, but he could feel the rungs of the ladder that he stood on deform under his feet and creak under their burden. The corner of a gunny sack was visible through the crack. Caldwell must have pulled a heavy sack of grain over the door to hide it. Standing on an upper rung of the fraidy hole's ladder, Blanche braced his back against the door and sawed at the corner of the sack with his axe. He opened a tiny hole, and a few seeds spilled out. With more effort, the hole widened, and the seed rushed out of the sack and fell into the depths of the fraidy hole. Blanche felt a charge of strength, and leaning harder into the door, was able to lift an opening that was wide enough for him to squeeze through. He rolled out and across the dirt floor of the barn. His sweat-drenched clothes gathered up the barn dust as if it were a magnet. It caked up like a shell. He looked at himself and thought he must look like a tar baby.

Peeking out the barn door, he could see that the slavecatcher had left the farm and was now on a road headed north in a buckboard pulled by two horses.

Blanche sat down on a stool. The hound licked at his face. "I sure wish I had a pup like you. Goodbye, Husband. Mind your master."

Blanche darted out of the barn with his axe.

"Hold on a bit, son," the farmer yelled after him. "It ain't safe yet."

It was too late. Nothing remained of Blanche except for the path of broken stalks of turkeyfoot that marked his trail into the tallgrass prairie.

16

— — —

Blanche woke the next morning with a start. For the second time, he'd dreamed of the Indian elder and his raccoon and crawfish story. It was a stupid story, and he wished he would forget about it. He stretched to loosen the stiffness in his bones, but he could do nothing to ease his hunger. He lifted his axe over his shoulder and headed out, north again, across the prairie.

The sun was high in the sky when he found a tiny trickle of water. He drank a bit and washed his body and clothes. His eyes followed the course of the tiny brook. Away in the distance, he could see the dark green line of trees. Beyond was that hazy ribbon of tall bluffs on the east bank of the Missouri River. The forest seemed too close for comfort. In all probability, a road ran near the river. A road meant traveling white folks, and Blanche had no reason to think that being seen by white folks was in his best interest.

He decided to set his path on a line that was parallel to the river. Blanche lost sight of the trees in the low places, and was only able to gauge his distance from the river when he crossed over a ridge.

As he crossed the brow of a rise, his eyes searched the horizon. He was startled to see that wagon tracks crossed his path less than a hundred yards away. Blanche's gaze followed them from the river bottom and into the prairie and to Thomason standing beside his buckboard. He had stopped on the road to pee.

Blanche and Thomason spotted one another in the same moment. He hollered, "Hold it right there!" Thomason jumped into his wagon, turned the horses, and slapped their flanks with the rein.

Blanche ran as fast as he could but Thomason overtook him easily. Blanche swung his axe for protection, but the big bully threw a loop of rope around his shoulders. As the fugitive fell to the earth, exhausted, the slavecatcher snatched the axe and buried the blade deep in the trunk of a tree.

Thomason shackled Blanche's wrists and ankles with chain and threw him, like a sack of potatoes, into the bed of the wagon. The buckboard sagged to one side as the big bully climbed into the driver's seat.

Thomason was triumphant. "I warted around with you long enough. I got pressing business back in

Lawrence. This will learn them bastards not to laugh at me."

Thomason reined his horses back onto the wagon tracks and to the river road. The trek southward led them straight into the wind. The horse followed the trail, and Thomason let him set his own, easy pace. He pulled a carpetbag from underneath the seat. Inside was a bottle of whiskey that he sipped from every so often, smacking his lips contentedly

As the buckboard made its way along the road, Blanche felt anger at himself for being so careless as to just walk up on his pursuer, and out in the middle of nowhere. He could blame weariness and hunger, but it was Blanche who was now in chains, not his weariness or hunger. Heavy iron rings bound his ankles, and those were connected by a short length of chain. They were designed to make walking possible but running difficult. He hadn't been shackled since that scary day when he was wrenched away from his mother. He supposed he'd take a beating or two on the way back to Westport. Then he thought about Spotted Face, the raccoon, and how he escaped, even took down his opponents, by tricking the crawfish into thinking he was dead.

The prairie road led to within shouting distance

of the forest that marked the course of the Missouri River. Blanche swallowed his hatred and broke a long silence. "It's sure dusty out on this old trail," he said.

"Yeah," Thomason said.

"Maybe you could get us both a sip of water before we get much farther."

Thomason took a big swig from his bottle. "Maybe."

"I sure is parched."

"Yeah."

"My throat is dry as a cow chip."

"Maybe one for the road." Thomason swigged on his bottle again.

"Seems like your old horses lost their gitty-up."

"There's nothing wrong with these old nags." Thomason took another sip.

"I sure is parched."

Thomason took another swig from the bottle. Blanche planned to get the driver drunk and then perhaps Thomason would drop his guard and that might give him an avenue of escape. At least for the moment, he was elated to think his plan had a chance of working.

Blanche babbled away as Thomason yielded to the influence of the whiskey. "You believe in ghosts?"

Thomason grunted. "Keep it quiet back there."

Blanche yawned. "No, sir, I don't believe in the

ghosties myself. Charms is one thing. But conjuring and witches. Do you believe in witches and ghosties?"

"No."

Blanche yawned again, bigger this time. "Yeah, me neither. I used to have a dime tied around my ankle with a raw cotton string. That right there will keep the ghosts away."

Thomason yawned. "Shut up now. I don't want to hear any more yapping from you."

"Yessir. The only reason a ghost shows himself to you is to show you where he hid his gold. You see a ghost and dig around where you seen him, and sure enough, if there's gold there, the ghost will disappear. Won't haunt that place no more. No more responsibility."

Blanche yawned. Thomason yawned.

"No, sir. Folks say there's a lot of ghosts at a graveyard, but I don't believe it. I sure wish I had my dime back."

Thomason was at his limit. He backhanded a big swinging paw at Blanche, yelling, "I told you to shut the hell up."

Blanche caught the punch on the shoulder. He rolled over the sideboard of the wagon bed and tumbled into the grass, shouting, "Pray mercy, Master. Sweet Jesus, I'm dead." He rolled on his side and lolled his tongue from his mouth, pretending to die. But he allowed an eyelid to ease open a slit. He watched as Thomason yanked on a lever to slam closed a brake.

Thomason shouted, "You better not die," and then he lurched off of the rig, catching the toe of his boot on the brake. His arms flailed as his heavy body fell toward the ground. He landed like a load of bricks on his belly. With a jerk, he straightened himself to his feet. A dead runaway wasn't worth a plug nickel. He bellowed into the wind, "You better not be dead, boy."

Quietly, moving only the hand farthest from Thomason, Blanche felt for a rock of a good size. A meaty hand grabbed him by the collar and pulled him to his feet. The fugitive swung the rock, and it found its mark on the jaw of the slavecatcher. The big man fell backward into the tallgrass.

Hope sprang in Blanche's chest. He found a larger rock and smashed it against the wagon wheel. Two spokes splintered and gave way, the wheel fell off the axle, and one side of the rig crashed to the earth. He slapped one horse on the flank, and since the brake had fallen away, the spooked horses were free to run. The horses were likely to harm themselves as they drug the busted-up rig around in circles.

Blanche ran north on the road, hobbled by his

shackles. He had to almost skip as the chain held his ankles too close together for a full stride. He looked back over his shoulder and saw that Thomason was reeling one way and then the other. Soon, Thomason was out of sight.

He was exhausted when he arrived at the site where Thomason had captured him, but he had renewed hope. Thomason hadn't caught up to him, which meant he hadn't even started out after him. He must have decided recapturing his horses was more important than getting Blanche—*at least for now,* Blanche thought—but his wagon was busted. The bully would be on foot.

Blanche found the tree with the embedded axe, pulled on the handle with all his might, and fell backward to the earth as the tree finally released the iron. He beat the locks in the chain open with his axe. The shackles fell away. Now he ran east, toward the green forest that lined the river. He ran through brush and over fallen timber. He thought he was making enough noise to raise the dead, but still he ran, through the jungle of undergrowth, toward the river, a mile, two miles, up to the river's edge. He couldn't run another step. His sides heaved to catch his breath. Blanche looked back through the snags of brush. No one followed his trail.

It was afternoon of the next day before Thomason reached the last farm he had passed. Two lame horses limped behind him, following on a lead. Caldwell's hound bayed to announce the slavecatcher's arrival. He found the old farmer slopping his hogs in the barnyard.

"Say, old timer," Thomason said.

"Say-o, son."

"You selling any horses today?"

"What happened, boy?"

"These damn Jayhawker horses. Both come up lame."

"Well, say-o, I got a sorrel stud," the farmer replied. "But I'd want three…uh…three hundred fifty for him. In trade."

"Three fifty's a heap of money."

"Worth every penny to a lard butt with nothing to trade but a couple of lame horses, I say-o."

"Something tells me I ain't got that much cash."

"If you're looking for a bargain, maybe you can just move on."

"I run into this stray a ways off."

"Stray?

"A fugitive."

"I see 'em here from time to time," Caldwell said. "Regular plague, I say-o."

"Just a kid, this one was. Been eating pretty high on the hog from the look of him," Thomason added. "Almost pudgy. I don't reckon you hid him out."

"No. Don't reckon I did, I say-o."

"I got you pegged as abolition. Sound on the goose, my ass."

"Umm…no."

Thomason reached across the slop trough, grabbed the farmer in one of his big mitts, and started cuffing the old man around.

"I don't know nothing about no colored boy."

"Did I say he was a boy?" Thomason asked. Where's the old woman?"

"Come on now, son, you ain't gonna mistreat an old woman, now, are you?"

"I just bet you got a fraidy hole here," Thomason said, entering the barn. He kicked aside a sack of grain that hid the trapdoor to the fraidy hole and grabbed the farmer by the collar. The hound barked angrily. "You played me for a fool, old man. Ain't no man gets away with that."

The farmer twisted free. "That's for cyclones. Now get the hell off'n my place. You seen what you come for."

Thomason threw a match down the hole. "Anymore of you fugitives hiding down there, come on out less'n you wants to be cooked up like a passel of roastin' ears." He tossed a handful of hay down the hole. It quickly caught fire and illuminated the inside of the fraidy hole.

Caldwell plead, "Listen, son, you can't do this. Don't do this."

Thomason answered sternly. "You abolition folks think you're not answerable. Always laughing. Let this be a lesson."

"I got a year's feed stored up in here. Everything I got."

Thomason struck another match and threw it on a dry pile of hay. The fire spread onto a pile of old rags.

The hound dog barked and ran in circles. Caldwell raced into the barn with a bucket of water. He was frantic. He threw the water on the blazing fire, but his effort was fruitless. The hound stood back, baying at the fire.

Thomason saddled Caldwell's sorrel, telling the farmer. "Send me a bill for the stud. And the pup too." He grabbed a length of rope from a corral post and tied it around the dog's neck. "This hound dog's going with me."

Thomason rode back to the road with the hound called Husband in tow.

17

— — —

Under a tree, Blanche tried to make a fire by striking his flint against the steel of his axe. Near the river, every bit of vegetation he found that looked like tinder was waterlogged. His task was hopeless.

The nighttime sounds that Blanche had become accustomed to on the prairie were swallowed up on the river bottom. Bullfrogs boomed over the dull whimper of rushing water. Crows mocked the owls until the beleaguered owls gained the upper hand after sunset. The sky was dark and cloudy. No Big Dipper showed the way. Blanche's head nodded, and his eyes drooped. He curled up in a fetal position beside a log and tried to sleep.

Blanche woke up. He was cold. The sky was brightening in the east. He rose and made his way back to the road beyond the tree line of the river.

He hid behind a giant cottonwood tree to look out for anyone on the road. So many fallen branches were on the ground around him, he couldn't tell if the tree was alive or dead. Above his head, he noticed that the tree had been stripped of its bark. The white scar of wood had been carved with symbols. *Indian symbols,* Blanche thought, but on closer inspection, he realized that one symbol going up the trunk was shaped like a footprint. Opposite the footprint symbols were round circles. Their meaning escaped the runaway, but they reminded him of something. He decided that the carvings resembled the footprints that old Aunt Shoe Peg left on the muddy path that led from the kitchen shack to the boarding house. That was it. On the left was a footprint, and on the right a circle represented the step of someone with a peg leg. The words of Reuben's "Drinking Gourd" song spoke out to him now:

> *The riverbank makes a very good road*
> *The dead trees will show you the way*
> *Left foot, peg foot, traveling on*
> *Follow the drinking gourd.*

A sign. The Underground Railroad. Blanche was elated. He pushed hard north now, trudging along the road, over one hill and the next, following the course of the river. The road grew more rutted with use with each mile he traveled. And soon, ahead, he could see rooftops and chimneys standing tall above a canopy of trees.

Blanche's walk slowed as he approached the river town of Nebraska City. In the window of a shack, he noticed a bow-tie-patterned quilt hanging from the window. He checked over each shoulder and then tramped around to the back of the house.

He found a cow penned beside a shed, and on a porch behind the shack, a middle-aged black woman shelled beans. She saw Blanche but refused to let herself make eye contact.

"Hello, Missus."

Still looking away, she asked him, "Have you ever been on the railroad?"

"I have been a short distance."

"Where did you start from?"

"The depot."

"Where did you stop?"

"At a place called safety."

The woman stood, picked up her crock of beans, and motioned Blanche inside the shack.

He sat at a crude table. The woman watched him eat with a stony eye. Her skin was so wrinkled, Blanche thought he could pour a cup of water on her head and none would run off.

"Mighty fine vittles, Aunt…"

"Folks round these parts call me Cow Woman."

"Cow Woman?"

"When Mistress died, I jumped on the back of that milk cow out back. Rode my cow all the way from Liberty, Missouri, to here in Nebraska City. Nothing but my Bible to keep me company."

"You didn't."

"Sure did. Ain't no one gonna stop a colored woman riding a milk cow, now, is they? My name's Delphie. Aunt Delphie."

The old woman chattered while she fitted Blanche out with a new change of clothes. She tied a bow tie around his neck and patted his chest.

"My mistress give me that name, Delphie. She taught me to card and spin cotton. Old Master, now he'd whip us good if he got mad. I got to choose the man I wanted to marry, though. Had to talk to my master about it first. He and the neighbor, man named Kinkaid, he owned my man, Joseph. Master had to get together with Kinkaid and talk it over. Master picked up that Bible there and told Joseph, he said, 'Now, Joseph, by God, if you ain't treating her right, by God, I'll take you up and whip you!' Then we jump over the broomstick, and we was married. Yessir. My man, Joseph Kinkaid, he worked on the railroad for his master. Worked hard. I chopped cotton in the morning then come back and nurse the children then go back to the field till dinner. Joe left me a widow ten years now. Master left my mistress a widow too. She treated us almost good as white folks. Give us coffee on Sunday morning. I can't say a hard word about her."

Auntie Delphie placed her hand on the book she carried in her sewing basket. "If my master seen me looking at this Bible, he would come up and say, 'What you know about reading a paper? Throw that down.' But I kept it when my mistress died. She didn't have no children. Willed me free."

Blanche picked up Aunt Delphie's precious book. It wasn't a Bible at all. It was an almanac. He hated Aunt Delphie's mistress for her cruelty. *How could you ever mistreat someone that way? This cow woman's so crazy she even thinks she loves you.*

"I'd have you reading in a few days," Blanche told her. "No sense in you staying an ignorant old field hand."

Aunt Delphie blustered up.

Blanche dug twenty dollars out of his wallet and gave it to her. He was gratified to see how much money he had left. He had supposed he would be running short by now, but so far, luck had been on his side. He was pretty proud of himself.

The old woman saw Blanche's freepapers in his wallet. "I'm free, and you're on the run. I don't care what those papers says. So who's ignorant?" She snatched up her sewing basket angrily. "The white trash conductor gets twenty dollars for a skiff."

A ragged pile of Blanche's dirty clothes littered the floor. Blanche peeled off another twenty dollars from the stash in his wallet. "Hope it's tight. I can't swim."

"Ignorant old field hand. I swan to goodness. I'm smarter than you. I don't have to risk life and limb on that old muddy river. I got my freepapers. I got duties here."

Blanche pushed his wallet into the place on his hip where a back pocket belonged. But there was no back pocket. His wallet fell onto the pile of his dirty, raggedy clothing.

The Big Dipper continued to call Blanche to freedom. It stood out like a beacon, high in the night sky over a log structure on the bank of the dark torrent of the Missouri River.

At ground level, Blanche was following a rifle-toting, scruffy white man. He was the conductor Aunt Delphie had told Blanche about, and his path led him and Blanche to the front of the unlit river-front building.

Inside a heavy door, the conductor lit a candle. He plodded after it, up a stair with Blanche behind. The dim light danced madly in the stairwell, but not a flicker lit the stair for Blanche. He could only follow, stumbling over the unseen steps, nearly dropping his axe. They found a small landing at the top of the stair. The conductor opened a door and a chilly draft blew out the flame. "It's cold, but you'll soon get a good warming," the conductor told him.

The upper room was dark, and when the conductor lit another match, Blanche saw that a coal oil lantern hung from a peg on the wall. The conductor touched the flame to the wick, and when the globe was closed and the flame burned bright, Blanche saw another man sitting across the room on a chair. His boots were off and he was rubbing his stocking-footed, aching feet.

Blanche looked around the room. The windows had bars.

Blanche quickly guessed that the man with the aching feet was the sheriff. Any doubt was erased when he told the conductor, "Looks like that reward is good as yours."

Blanche swung his axe without hesitation, and the conductor dodged away, piling onto the sheriff. A pistol discharged. Blanche raced out of the room and toward the dark stairwell. Another shot rang out, this one from the conductor's rifle. It sounded like a canon and echoed in the narrow stairwell.

Blanche felt splinters of wood spray his neck as he plunged down the dark shaft.

At the bottom, he pushed against the door he'd come in. Locked, it wouldn't budge. Light shone out from under another door at the foot of the stair. Blanche threw his shoulder into the door and it sprung open. He found himself in a room fitted out like a personal residence where a woman, evidently the sheriff's wife, darned stockings by the light of a lantern. Two little kids sat up in bed, and the sheriff's wife yelled bloody murder. "Help! Help! He'll kill us all!"

The children screamed like banshees. Seeing himself as cornered now, Blanche swung his axe at a Franklin stove, and when he struck it flush, the stove skidded off of its brick deck and spilled onto its side. Embers scattered across the wooden floor.

Blanche smashed open a window with his axe and wrestled through the opening to freedom.

The sheriff's family squalled out loudly enough to raise the dead. "Eeeeeeek! Eeeeeeek!" The wife screeched like a wounded bobcat, while the children yelled, "Papa! Fire! Mama!"

The sheriff and conductor galumphed into the room after their prisoner. The stocking-footed sheriff soon found himself dancing on burning embers. The conductor tussled with a ramrod, intent on reloading his muzzle-loader. "My five hundred!" he hollered.

"Ye gods," the sheriff yelled back, skipping in a circle. "He's burnt the jailhouse to the ground."

The conductor could scarcely hear him over the shouts of the sheriff's family. "Eeeeeeek! Eeeeeeek! Papa! Fire! Mama!"

Blanche tumbled down the back of the jailhouse. It backed up to the river bank, so the ground below the window was much lower than he expected. And muddy. He had difficulty walking. His feet sank deep into the mushy ground on the river bank.

Blanche stumbled over a log. He picked it up and heaved it into the torrent with a great splash.

The conductor bounded around the back corner of the jailhouse and stood below Blanche's escape window.

"My five hundred!" he yelled and, cocking his rifle, aimed at a target in the rushing water beyond. Over the shrieks of the sheriff's wife and children, rifle fire roared across the dark water. The rifle kicked hard and threw the conductor backward. He landed on his fanny on the muddy bank.

The footsore sheriff waddled around the corner of the jailhouse to the riverbank. "You kill your five hundred?"

"Winged him, I reckon."

"Get in here and help me put this fire out." The sheriff and the conductor scrambled up the bank, around and into the front of the log house.

Beyond their vision, Blanche ran south, back across the river road and into the dark prairie, carrying his axe, the drinking gourd at his back.

18

— — —

It was daybreak and Blanche awoke in the cleft of a hollow tree. He felt for his wallet and realized it was missing. *Lost to that double-dealing, back-stabbing old Cow Woman, sure as this world.* He knew the odds against making it to Detroit were slim without money or even fake freepapers, but most of all, he was angry for letting himself get tricked by an ignorant field hand.

Travel near the river was nearly impossible. In the afternoon, he heard a chilling sound. The far-off baying of a hound that told him it was time to make tracks. *That old Cow Woman continues to sell me out!*

He worked his way as fast as he could through underbrush to the river's edge. The river would take him away faster than he could run. He wrestled a dead log into the muddy stream and jumped in after it with his axe.

The makeshift raft was waterlogged, and it sank in the river like a rock in a cistern. He struggled to keep his head above the water as he pushed away from the sinking log. Water washed over his head and rushed into his throat when he tried to breathe. He fought against the torrent and his feet touched the bottom. He scrambled back to shore, coughing muddy water from his lungs.

Thomason sat on horseback on a low bank above him. Blanche could still hear the hound baying in the distance.

"Well looky here what I found," Thomason said, drawing his pistol. "Son, you leave a trail as wide as a buffalo."

Without giving himself time to think, Blanche sprang up the bank and with a scream— "Yaaaaaaaaaah!"—threw a handful of sand and rocks into the face of the sorrel stud horse that Thomason rode.

The horse bucked just as Thomason fired his pistol. The shot missed its mark. The sorrel began to buck and kick. The slavecatcher bore down a second pistol on Blanche, but this shot misfired. While Thomason struggled to avoid getting pitched into the river by the bucking horse, Blanche darted off downriver and into a mucky, overgrown, swampy backwater.

Thomason dismounted and grabbed the reins of his horse. The steed slowly calmed down. "Where's my damn dog?" he shouted at the horse.

He tied the horse to a branch and reloaded his pistols. He whistled loudly through his teeth, and then yelled upriver, "Hey, you dumb-butt Yankee mongrel!"

Out of the bushes, covered with cockleburs, Caldwell's biscuit-eating blue tick hound came loping to Thomason's side. "Go git him, Husband. Sic," Thomason told him.

The hound sat on the riverbank and licked his groin.

"I'm thinking to change your name to Atchison," the slavecatcher told the hound. "Some damn tracking hound you are."

Thomason kicked at the hound, slipped, and fell to the ground on the muddy riverbank. Smeared with mud, he mounted his horse and urged the beast to follow Blanche's path off into the muck. The hound bayed and charged off in the same direction.

The hound ran past Thomason like his horse was tied to a post. The slavecatcher eased his mount slowly into the snaky backwater marsh where the fugitive had disappeared.

Ahead of the slavecatcher, Blanche crashed through the sludge that choked the backwater slough near the river. He heard the baying of the hound and pressed ahead.

He was already dead tired from slogging through the swamp. When he slowed to catch his breath, he heard the hound and realized that he seemed much closer now. Ahead of him, his way was blocked by a waterway and, on the other side, a tangle of fallen timber.

Struggling through water up to his neck, Blanche made his way across the small channel to the knot of logs. He found a break that he could squeeze through and hid behind the snags to catch his breath.

The sound of the baying of the hound was louder now, closer. Husband emerged from underbrush to find the channel. He raced back and forth along the water's edge, baying at the top of his lungs.

The hound's attention was focused on the knot of limbs, and Blanche knew he'd been spotted. Husband's tail wagged happily, and he plunged into the slough. He paddled like crazy across the channel, swimming ever closer to Blanche's hiding place.

When Husband reached the far side, he tried to climb the knot of logs. Unable to get any traction, he swam between the break where his prey was hidden. He licked at Blanche's face and wagged his tail, ecstatic to have found his long-lost friend.

Blanche tried to hold the dog's mouth closed, but each time he managed to twist his muddy muzzle free and bay. "I'm sorry, Husband, I'm so sorry," Blanche told him. He grabbed the collar around the hound's neck and pulled him underwater. The baying stopped, but Husband thrashed about, resisting Blanche.

"I'm sorry, boy. I'm sorry. Go on."

Blanche held Husband underwater until he ceased to struggle for life. Tears filled the fugitive's eyes. His heart was as empty as it had been the day he was snatched away from his mother.

From his hiding place in the tangle of stumps, Blanche watched Thomason prowl the banks of the slough. "Where you at, you damn hound?"

Thomason looked to the ground. Even Blanche could see the paw prints Husband had left in the mud. The slavecatcher trailed the dog back-and-forth along the bank of the slough. Finally he steered away, toward the river's edge, and didn't return.

Blanche dragged himself across the channel in the slough and pulled himself out on the mud bank beyond. He was covered in slime. He took off north, doubling back on his tracker. Before long, he was back at the river road on the edge of the prairie. He looked both ways and then darted into the tallgrass on the west side of the road.

He was walking north again, wet from hiding in the swamp and drenched in feelings of despair and anguish. *Poor Husband, he didn't want nothing but to be my friend*. Blanche sat down in the tallgrass and cried for the first time since he'd crossed the Mississippi. Tears rolled down his cheeks. He kept seeing the happy, flop-eared Husband in his mind's eye, wagging his tail, jumping up and down, just delighted to be alive and to have a friend. For the time being he was free, but the future seemed so dark to Blanche, darker than midnight.

19

— — —

He plodded across the rolling prairie until long past sundown. The night was moonless. One foot forward, then the next—his march was grinding and mechanical. He imagined himself as a printing press. Forward, again and again, machinelike, soulless, hopeless. Poor Husband. Exhaustion tore at his body.

What he thought was a tear in his eye began to look like a spot of light from out of the gloom. When he tramped closer, the light became a lantern in the window of a sod house.

Not far from the house, Blanche caught sight of a haystack silhouetted against the night sky. Everything was quiet, and the haystack offered warmth and comfort. He burrowed into the hay…and discovered another occupant. Blanche yelped.

"I'm coming out," the voice said, trembling in fear. "I'm just a poor hungry country preacher. I ain't armed." Blanche recognized his voice from the boarding house. The other guest making a bed in the haystack was the preacher Butler.

The preacher hidden in the hay obviously was more frightened by Blanche than Blanche was by him. "Don't come out on my account. Is there room for one more in there?"

"Get in here, son."

Blanche crawled into the haystack. "I'm so hungry I'd eat a skunk," he said.

"Here's some cob nuts I stole from a mouse's nest. I got a few wild grapes if you want them."

"Preacher, huh?"

Blanche mulled over the vow he'd made to himself, the one about turning and walking away from the next preacher he met. His attention returned to the cob nuts and grapes. "Methodist," Butler told him.

"Me too. I never knew a body could get so hungry." Blanche remembered that this preacher had been fair with him in the boarding house and didn't seem so bad. He decided to shelve his plans. He promised himself that he would confront the next preacher he met. One would surely come along when he wasn't so busy pushing wild grapes into his face. He ate like a convicted man.

"Where you headed?"

Blanche yawned. "I had it in my mind to head east across the river, then Detroit. Figure to make my way to either Canada or Toronto. Now I'm not so sure…" His words became snores.

Smoke curled into the morning sky from a stovepipe on the roof of the sod house. The dwelling looked a lot like the Kanza lodges except that it was smaller and put down a rectangular footprint on the prairie. Grass sprouted from the rooftop.

The preacher had still not seen the face of the boy who slept in the haystack with him. They had talked between themselves and had nearly decided to approach the house and ask for food when, peeking out of the haystack, they saw a rider on a big sorrel stud. It was Thomason, the slavecatcher. He dismounted and tied his mount to a fencepost. Without pause, he snatched up a couple of fat hens, wrung their necks, and stuffed them into his saddlebags. Then he approached the doorway of the sod house and pounded on it as if he wanted to knock it off its hinges. "Folks, I just come to find out if anyone's been hiding fugitives around these parts. Come on out, I ain't a gonna hurt yah none."After a brief moment, he climbed atop the sod house and kicked over the stovepipe chimney. Smoke boiled out of gaps around the window frames of the house.

Soon, a woman and a girl—Blanche guessed the young one was about his age—threw open the door, spilling out of the sod house, coughing and wheezing from the smoke that had been loosed inside when Thomason kicked over the chimney. Mother and daughter both shrieked in fear. The woman, armed with a musket but blinded by smoke, fired the rifle at nothing. She began to swing the muzzle-loader like an axe to fend off the attacker she couldn't see. Flames licked out the doorway.

Thomason grabbed the woman and easily disarmed her. Then he seized the girl and tied them together to a post. "Folks say you been harboring fugitives. If that's so, I'm going to carve him up like a beef. I might carve on you too, if you don't give him up." He drew his Bowie knife and slowly, malevolently, laughing like a jackass, menaced the women, sawing the buttons from the upper part of their dresses with the tip of his long knife. He ripped down the bodices, leaving the womenfolk bare breasted.

Thomason grinned and stepped inside the house. He returned with a firebrand in one hand and a smoldering, orange-hot branding iron in the other. "You got any more firearms?" he asked.

"If I did, you'd be toes to the sky," the woman told him. "You heathen."

The slavecatcher's eyes were red from the smoke and filled with tears. "We'll see if this doesn't get you tell me the truth," Thomason said. Wiping his eyes on his forearm, he pressed the branding iron on the woman's upper arm. Smoke billowed from her flesh as it burned under the hot iron. She and her daughter cried out to the heavens, "Save us, Lord."

"You wouldn't have a stray hiding in a haystack now, would yah?"

While the slavecatcher's bleary eyes enjoyed the torment of the womenfolk, Blanche stole from the haystack to a corner the sod house, out of Thomason's sight.

The daughter shouted out, "Oh, Father," and the slavecatcher turned his head to the road.

"Who's there," he shouted, supposing the girl was calling to someone behind him.

In that moment, Blanche darted from his hiding place and untied the horse's rein from the post. He slapped the sorrel on the flank.

Thomason whirled around when he heard the hoof beats to see his horse bolting straightaway into the prairie. He dropped his instruments of torture. His horse and saddle, to say nothing of his supper, was headed to the horizon. Thomason broke and ran after his goods.

When the slavecatcher was out of sight, Blanche loosed the bonds of the screaming womenfolk.

"It's you. He's after you," the mother said. "You

brought this on us. Runaway!" She said the word like a curse. The womenfolk grabbed their ragged clothes around themselves and together they ran to hide in the tallgrass.

Butler trotted from the haystack, and together he and Blanche scrambled to the top of a wall of the burned-out sod house. The roof had been supported by wooden timbers that had burned, so it had fallen in and smothered the fire. They set their eyes on the prairie, searching for some sign of the woman and her daughter.

The runaway's heart was heavy for the mistreatment that the slavecatcher handed out to the white women, and would continue to—he knew that Thomason would be back. If he had never run away, this misfortune would never have fallen at their doorstep.

"Halloooo!" Butler shouted into the tallgrass. Then to Blanche, "I think they're gone. Say...ain't you that kid from Westport? You a runaway?"

"I don't know if I am or I ain't. Come on, let's get out of here."

"That slavecatcher was either after you or he wasn't. Which is it?"

"Marse Henry always told me I was free when he died. He got himself whacked in the head with an axe handle. The way I got it figured, I'm free. Let's go."

Butler's eyes searched the grassland again for the womenfolk. "They're plumb gone. Poor souls."

"I hoped we'd get at least a bowl of grits," Blanche said.

The preacher and the runaway clambered down from the roof. Together they walked toward the road without exchanging words.

Once there, Butler turned north, upriver.

"Good luck to you, preacher," Blanche said. "But I think I'm gonna head back downriver."

"That don't make sense."

"I met an Indian guy who offered me a reasonable proposition."

"The closest town is upriver," the preacher said, and Blanche thought it over. "You'll never find your Indian."

Blanche rubbed his chin in silence.

"I guess you like the way those Indians cook grits," Butler said. "That slavecatcher went that away. You better head this away with me."

Butler was right. Blanche didn't want to eat buffalo and berries the rest of his life, and the best way to distance himself from Thomason was to continue north. Blanche caught up with the preacher and together they headed upriver.

The haystack had been a comfortable bed, but it was short on food. By the time the sun was high in the sky, both men were dead tired and hungry. Both of them stumbled as they worked just to put one foot in front of the other on the uneven roadway. They stopped for a drink of water from a prairie creek that meandered into the jungle of the river bottom.

"That slavecatcher and all his ilk, they's gonna have a rude awaking when the day of the Lord arrives," Butler said.

"I reckon it's their raising—it's what they've been taught."

"Taught to burn houses and barns? Taught to sack free state towns? What school teaches that?"

Blanche answered Butler testily. "White folks school, I reckon. I've never been to school, so I'm not sure."

"They murder free state men and mutilate their bodies. They ravish the women folks. You saw it yourself. They brand innocents like livestock. Turn them out on the prairie, completely naked. Common practice. You saw it with your own eyes."

"They been doing that to Negroes a long time now."

"What about the preachers being accosted?"

"That too."

"Church house doors nailed shut?"

"Negroes don't have church houses to nail shut."

"Well then, what about the printing presses, throwing them in the river and all?"

"Never heard of that. What happened?" Blanche was keen to hear about this. Printing presses were almost sacred to him.

"That pompous ass Atchison, him and that no account postmaster. Led a gang into Parkville. They throwed the presses and all the type in the river. They did. Run the publisher and the printer clean out of the county."

"Hadn't heard about that…"

"Yeah, and they tarred and feathered me and Phillips, you remember him, a railroad lawyer."

Blanche nodded.

"They splotched us with hot tar and threw chicken feathers on us, and then they rode us out of town on a fence rail. All the way to the river, set us adrift, they did. Just for talking abolition."

"You should see the scars on slaves' backs. Ever seen that? You never seen a brand on a black man?"

"They've defrauded the free state folks of fair elections."

"Now that I think about it, Negroes don't have printing presses, and they sure as hell don't have elections."

Butler was stunned. "We're all in this together."

"Not me. It's not my fight. If you white folks want to fight about it, go ahead on. I got my hands full, just fighting for Blanche Bruce, and all I know is I'm sick of running."

Few words were exchanged between the preacher and the runaway as they made their way north along the river road.

20

— — —

Blanche had mixed feelings about heading north with Butler. He didn't understand how the preacher could be so prickly about the treatment the abolition folks were receiving and at the same time blind to the troubles of slaves. Any slave would trade places with any white man any day of the week. Even the rough going on the rutted roadway was considerably easier than it was out on the prairie. On the river bottom, the land was mostly flat, and near the road, the tallgrass was beaten down. A black boy walking alone on the prairie stuck out like a sore thumb, but walking along a road with a white man, Blanche knew, he wouldn't raise an eyebrow.

In the afternoon, as Blanche and Butler trudged along the roadway, they spotted a horse and buckboard wagon ahead, tied to a bush near a thicket of sand plums.

"You don't suppose it's the slavecatcher?" Butler asked.

"The one that's after me had a buckboard, but the last time I saw it, it wasn't in very good condition, so I kind of doubt it," Blanche said.

"Well, good. I'm itching to tell someone about them settlers getting burned out."

"If I was you, I'd keep it under my hat a spell."

"It's the truth. I saw it with my own eyes. So did you."

"I got a gut feeling that one of the big reasons you're walking is that you don't know when to keep your mouth shut."

"Yeah, I reckon," the preacher conceded. They shortened their strides and slowed as they approached the buckboard.

A man stepped out of the thicket with a bucket filled with fresh-picked sand plums. Blanche recognized his features. It was the corrupt conductor from Nebraska City, the turncoat that wanted to turn him in for the reward. Surprised to see people, he fumbled and dropped the bucket. His mess of sand plums spilled across the roadway. He pulled a pistol from under his belt and demanded, "What we got here?"

"Listen, Mister," Butler told him, "we ain't going to do you no harm. I'm just a poor country preacher, broke and hungry."

The conductor gave Blanche a real good look,

unsure whether he recognized the runaway slave boy he'd only seen in the dark. "Folks here in Nebraska Territory don't really cotton much to preachers holding slaves."

Butler winked at Blanche. "We're passing through."

"Load up, then," the conductor told them as he picked up the scattered plums. "Give you a ride into town." Butler claimed a front seat next to the conductor.

"Don't mind if we do. In the back, boy."

Blanche gave Butler a steely-eyed glare before crawling in the wagon bed. He might have to play the part of slave for the time being, but he didn't want the preacher to cabbage on to any ideas.

The conductor shared his canteen and the sand plums with Blanche and Butler. He whistled tunes and told a tall tale or two in a big, booming voice. He didn't seem to be able to talk without shouting. Perhaps he thought his riders were deaf. He was far too hilarious for Blanche's comfort, and the runaway decided that it was best to suppose that the conductor recognized him.

Butler was relaxed, enjoying being off his feet and the patches of shade they drove through on the prairie road beside the river. He had no idea that the conductor and the runaway might have met before. Blanche didn't want the conversation to turn to politics or fugitive slaves. *Get him talking about farming,* Blanche pleaded silently with Butler. He caught Butler's eye and gestured to him with finger to his lips, "hush, you," and to emphasize his point, he balled up his fist like an Irish prizefighter and shook it at the preacher.

To Blanche's great relief, the conductor seemed to hate the sound of anyone else's voice. Blanche was relieved to see him interrupt every time the preacher tried to talk. All the while, Blanche noticed that one of the conductor's eyes kept rolling back to check on his cargo. When their eyes met in an uneasy stare, the conductor turned away and started singing.

> *Get out of the way for Old Dan Tucker*
> *He's too late to get his supper*
> *Supper's over, dishes waw-ershed*
> *All that's left is a piece of squaw-ersh.*

"Hey, preacher, how'd you like that one. Pretty good, huh?"

"I suppose."

The conductor twisted around again to eyeball Blanche. "What'd yah think, kid?"

"Never heard better."

"Come on and sing with me, preacher. This is my lucky day."

Old Dan Tucker was a fine old man
Washed his face in a frying pan
Combed his hair with a wagon wheel
Died with a toothache in his heel.

Blanche didn't want this to be a lucky day for the big loudmouth. The conductor's Bowie knife hung at his hip, inviting mischief.

Get out of the way for Old Dan Tucker
He's too late to get his supper
Supper's over, breakfast's cooking
Old Dan Tucker...

21

— — —

Behind them they heard a voice holler out, "Hal-oooo!" They all saw Thomason at the same time, just as he spurred his horse into a gallop and charged in their direction. He must have caught the sorrel. Blanche was beyond fearful. Now he was angry. *If I'm going down, I'm going down armed.* He snatched the conductor's Bowie knife and dove out of the wagon and into the underbrush.

As Thomason gained ground on the wagon, the conductor pulled on his reins and jammed on the brake. "Whoa! Whoa!" He scrambled to retrieve a pistol that was cinched under his belt.

Thomason rode up alongside the wagon. "Where's the fugitive? Where did he go?"

"He's the runaway?" the conductor said. "I knew it!"

Thomason spurred his horse into the brush.

From above and behind him, Blanche leapt from a tree limb onto Thomason's back. He bit Thomason's ear, hard, and Thomason yelped like a girl.

Thomason's weight shifted, and the horse bucked. The slavecatcher and Blanche tumbled to the ground, unhorsed.

They rolled to a stop on the ground. Blanche was on top. He pressed the conductor's Bowie knife into a sweaty fold of skin under Thomason's chin.

"Say your prayers, pattyroller!" Blanche felt he was conjuring old Reuben's fighting spirit.

"Hold on there!"

Thomason and Blanche looked up to see the conductor. He had the drop on the wrestlers. He held his shotgun on them at point blank range.

"Don't shoot him," Thomason said. "He ain't worth nothing dead."

Butler took Thomason's pistol.

"I was thinking about shooting you," the conductor said. "The kid's mine."

"Don't waste your powder, mister," Blanche said. "I'm going to cut his gizzard out."

With the sound of a mechanical click, the conductor realized that the game was now more complicated. Butler held a pistol to his temple.

"Well, I swan to goodness," Butler said. "If that kid belongs to anyone, he belongs to me. I'm telling you, kid, don't do it."

Blanche eased off. He got up off of Thomason's chest and took the conductor's shotgun. "Old Man

Henry used to say, 'God made man, but Sam Colt made 'em equal.' You," he told the conductor, "tie that horse to the wagon."

As he hitched Thomason's horse to the tailgate of his wagon, the conductor spoke up. "They hang horse thieves around these parts. You might oughta think about that, preacher."

"Yeah," Thomason said. "So just give me my pistol back."

Thomason stood up under Blanche's guard, and Blanche felt compelled to tell him, "Thomason, if you move a peg in my direction, you won't live to regret it."

"I'll give you a brand-new shiny silver dollar. What do you think about that?"

"The guns aren't for sale," Blanche told him.

"We'll let you go. Run anywhere you want. As fast as you want. Free as birds. You can trust us."

"You think we can trust 'em?" Butler asked Blanche.

"I wouldn't trust him as far as I can smell him. Now, both of you. Off with the boots. Throw 'em up here in the back. And if either of you looks cross-eyed, I'll empty this scattergun into one of you and slice the gullet out of the one left standing."

"Listen, kid," Thomason told him, "just give us the guns. You're going to get yourself hurt."

"That's a chance I'm willing to take. Now put your boots in the wagon bed, like I said. And take the saddle off the horse and throw it in the bed."

Thomason loosened the cinch around the horse's belly and heaved his saddle into the wagon bed.

"Get to walking. And step up the pace."

Thomason muttered, "I'll chase you to the ends of the earth."

Blanche's brow knitted with anger at Thomason's threat. "Fine. Now your drawers. Get 'em off. Both of you." Blanche pointed the shotgun at Thomason.

As Thomason and the conductor dropped their drawers and threw them in the wagon bed, Butler chimed in. "If you shot the slavecatcher between the eyes, I couldn't lay blame."

Blanche considered Butler's suggestion. "You know, Thomason, me and the preacher, we saw you and your bunch burn out that bunch of sodbusters."

"So you say."

"Saw it with my own eyes," Butler said, raising his hand to the sky. "As God is my witness."

"I suspected they was harboring fugitives."

"Well, how come you ripped their clothes off?" Blanche asked. "And how come you branded them?"

"You branded women?" the conductor asked.

"I was in hot pursuit."

"Nebraska Territory don't much cotton to barn burning Missouri pukes," the conductor said.

"You need to skedaddle back to Douglas County, Thomason," Blanche told him. "'Cause if you're standing there in another minute, I'm going to skin you alive."

Thomason snapped the reins of his horse away from the tailgate of the wagon. He tried in vain to mount the horse bareback.

"Now get to cracking," Blanche told the conductor. "And if you want to keep those long johns on, I better not hear any back sass."

The stocking-clad conductor led out. Butler drove the wagon, and Blanche kept the firearms trained on the conductor.

Behind them, the barefoot Thomason gave up on his attempt to mount his horse bareback. He began walking south, leading his horse.

22

— — —

The conductor's wagon trundled into town led by its barefoot owner, stripped to his long underwear. Blanche and Butler sat side-by-side in the driver's seat. The young man cradled the conductor's shotgun in his lap.

They drove past Aunt Delphie's shack. She was sitting out front, and Blanche cast a cold stare in her direction. "That old biddy sold me down the river," he told Butler under his breath.

The sheriff of Nebraska City sat in a rocking chair on a boardwalk in front of his office, his bandaged feet propped on a rail. "Red!" he hollered out at the conductor. "What in the blue-eyed wide world is going on here?" The sheriff took another gander at Blanche, as Butler steered the team to a trough of water in front of the sheriff's office.

The conductor stepped gingerly into the trough to soak his feet. The sheriff rubbed his chin. "I'm waiting for someone to offer to tell me why Red is barefoot and stripped down to his long johns." Butler allowed the team to drink, but Blanche kept the shotgun trained on the conductor.

Aunt Delphie arrived on foot. Other townsfolk collected around the sheriff's office, some curious, some concerned, others angry. Black men weren't supposed to brandish weapons.

The conductor burst out, "Someone grab that boy!"

The sheriff had other ideas. "I'll do the telling someone to grab someone's around here. Someone grab that boy."

But Blanche turned the scattergun on the crowd, and the townsmen melted back.

"Ain't you same boy who set my jailhouse on fire?" the sheriff asked him.

"He's the same one," the conductor said.

"I'm Blanche Bruce, and I'm turning in my prisoner."

"What crimes you charging him with?"

"For stealing the twenty dollars I gave him for a skiff."

"That kid's a fugitive," the conductor shouted, "and he's mine. Everyone knows that possession is nine whatchamacallits."

"If he's yours, Red," the sheriff said, "then you take the shotgun away."

The conductor lifted his feet out of the trough and walked gingerly in Blanche's direction.

Just then, Delphie stepped in, wrenched the shotgun out of Blanche's grip, and with a swift kick, put a heavy boot in the conductor's fanny.

"You big tub of lard, you leave that boy alone. This boy, he's as free as I am. He's got as much right to buy a skiff as anybody if he has money. Boy, read that paper to 'em. Tell 'em what it says." She handed Blanche his lost wallet and the forged freepapers.

Blanche glared at Delphie as if to say "keep your mouth shut," but she shoved the freepapers into his fist. "Now do what your Aunt Delphie says. Read the dang paper."

"It ain't you that's gonna take a whipping."

Now Delphie swung the shotgun around in an arc, and the crowd moved back a step.

A merchant voiced what all the townspeople were thinking. "You can't do that," the merchant shouted out.

"Anyone whips you, it's over my dead body. Now read, I say."

So Blanche read, and as he did, the townspeople grew silent. "'This is to make known to all whom it may concern, that Blanche Kelso Bruce, the bearer of this paper, is a free boy. He was put with me to learn the carpenter's trade in Sedalia. He lived with me some six years. I have universally found him to be strictly honest and strictly observes the truth, has never been put much to joining carpenter work…'"

"What's that prove?" the conductor interrupted.

"Everyone know a slave can't read," Delphie said. "He's free." The townspeople murmured.

"Dang it, Slick. I had my mitts on this kid a week ago. He set your jailhouse on fire. The law's on my side."

"What law?"

"Finder's keepers."

"You told me you shot that one."

"Well, I did. Winged him anyway."

"Red, this kid ain't got a mark on him."

It was as if every man and woman who had gathered around to watch chose this time to speak his or her piece, until a high-pitched voice cut through the racket. "I had him first anyhow!" It was Butler.

The sheriff lifted his hat, scratched the back of his head, and asked, "Just who in the Sam Hill are you?"

"I'm the Reverend Pardee Butler, and I took custody of that there boy my own self."

"That's my five hundred," the conductor bawled.

"He's mine, I tell you!"

The sheriff rubbed his whiskered chin. "Looks to

me like the preacher has priority. If he's slave, he belongs to the preacher. And if he's free, Red, you need to quit molesting him."

"And you, cheating a boy out of twenty dollars," Aunt Delphie swaggered. "Oh, Lordy, the patty-rollers would love to hear about a man selling a boat to a kid he thinks is runaway."

The conductor collected the reins of team, and twisting his face into a frown, climbed into the seat of his buckboard. The crowd of people choked around the wagon.

"Boy," the sheriff asked Blanche. "You know this woman?"

"She's my aunt. Hey, you aren't gonna set that man free now are you? He still has my twenty dollars!"

"You got twenty dollars, Red?"

The conductor turned back. "Why?"

"Pay the kid his twenty dollars."

Blanche felt thunderstruck. He'd been wrong about Aunt Delphie and the sheriff too. He was honest after all. *Maybe I'm wrong about a few other things*, he thought.

The conductor found his trousers in the bed of the wagon and the wallet that was in a hip pocket. He reluctantly pulled out some bank notes and handed them to the runaway.

"Nuh-uh," Blanche said, refusing the paper money. "I paid you gold."

The conductor wiped his nose on the back of his index finger and gave it a tug. He returned the paper to his wallet and found a twenty-dollar gold piece in his pocket. Handing over the coin to Blanche with an angry glare, he said, "That's my shotgun."

Blanche discharged the shotgun into the sky and returned it to the conductor.

Blanche, Butler, and Aunt Delphie walked toward the little shack with the milk cow out back. Thomason's pistol and Bowie knife were stuffed under the young man's belt.

"It weren't me what told you out," Delphie said. "It was that white trash conductor. Was him went over for the reward."

Blanche understood. "Aunt Delphie, I'm sorry. I shouldn't have ever called you ignorant."

"Would you look at that nice new suit of clothes? Land sakes."

"I went swimming."

Aunt Delphie's voice was serious now. "There's work here needs doing."

"Don't look at me. I'm going on across with the preacher."

"Not without a hot meal, you don't. Crossing over can just wait till tomorrow."

The next morning, Blanche, Butler, and Delphie eased down a muddy, sloping roadway that led to a quay on the river. The path was lined by poles laid on the earth, buried halfway in the ground, skids that would help men move heavy freight from the quay to the town above.

Delphie was telling Blanche for the tenth time, "Once you get yourself across the river, head north to a town called Tabor. Look for Reverend Todd."

"Why don't you come and show me the way?"

"I got a place here. I have my duties. You go on."

"You're free. You can go anywhere you want."

"Boy, if'n I ain't helping folks, my freedom ain't worth a cold bucket of spit."

Below them on the quay, men unloaded freight from a steamboat. They struggled with heavy boxes. As Blanche got closer, he recognized Sam Wood, the fighting Quaker, and Colonel Lane. Already, two heavy boxes had been offloaded. Three similar crates were stacked on the boat's deck. Big block letters on the side of the boxes read, *BIBLES*.

Blanche was delighted to see the Quaker. His throat nearly seized up, but he managed to exhale and say, "Mr. Wood. It's good to see you looking well," and with a wary eye on Lane, he added, "both of you."

"Blanche. Friend." Wood grabbed Blanche and gave him a big bear hug. "Where you headed?"

Blanche was startled by an outward gesture of affection from a white man, and he looked around to see if anyone else had noticed. "Dubuque, I reckon," he said, so that no one else could hear.

"Need a Bible? Compliments of Mr. Beecher."

Blanche was elated. It would be the first book he ever owned. "Could I?"

Wood pried back the lid on the box. Blanche reached in eagerly and then quickly withdrew his hand. The Bible crate was full of grease-covered Sharpe's rifles.

"On second thought," Wood said, "I think the militia in Lawrence might not like it if one of their Bibles came up missing."

Butler had already seated himself in a flat-bottomed boat. "Come on, Blanche."

"Mrs. Wood says Jesus said, 'Blessed are the peace-makers,'" Blanche said.

Colonel Lane chimed in, "Yeah, well, Jesus also said, 'I did not come to bring peace, but a sword.'"

"God be with you, friend," Wood told Blanche, as

the men returned to the struggle of offloading the heavy boxes onto dry land.

Blanche boarded the skiff with Butler.

Delphie dabbed at her eyes with a handkerchief and prayed, "Swing low, sweet chariot," as if the little skiff were a fiery chariot sent by the Lord to carry Blanche to the Iowa bluffs and freedom beyond the Missouri River.

Blanche pulled on the oars and the skiff headed into the stream. Delphie yelled across the water, "Take care yourself now, you hear?"

"I'll write…" *Lord, how stupid can I be? She can't read it if I do write.* Blanche bowed his head in shame. He doubled his stroke, and the boat skimmed across the swirling, scouring river that separated him from freedom on the far shore.

Tears welled up in his eyes. He sang and rowed to the beat of his song.

> *Well if I could I surely would*
> *Stand on the rock where Moses stood*
> *Pharaoh's army got drown-ded*
> *O Mary don't you weep.*

Butler's voice entered on the chorus.

O Mary don't you weep, don't you mourn
O Mary don't you weep, don't you mourn
Pharaoh's army got drown-ded
O Mary don't you weep.

Well Mary wore three links of chain
On every link was freedom's name
Pharaoh's army got drown-ded
O Mary don't you weep.

Brothers and sisters don't you cry
There'll be good times by and by
Pharaoh's army got drown-ded
O Mary don't you weep.

Butler clambered onto a sandbar on the eastern shore and with a whispered "Praise the Lord," tugged the nose of the skiff out of the water. Steep bluffs rose above them. The Iowa side had none of the improvements that the town fathers of Nebraska City had built on the western shore. He tied the boat to a snag and saw that Blanche remained at the oars, deep in his thoughts, looking back across the river at Sam Wood, Colonel Lane, and Aunt Delphie.

A fighting Quaker. The Lord sure enough picks some strange ducks. Back in Westport, when Henry and his big-talking friends lit up the cigars, they always pegged the free soil Kansas folks as a bunch cowards. *"Jayhawkers! Cowards!" If I heard it once, I heard it a thousand times. But no one's ever going to nail Sam Wood's church house shut. No sir. Looks like to me he'd fight a circle saw. Henry might have had to think again if he had ever ran into Sam Wood. A sure enough fighter if I ever saw one.*

Blanche remembered a picture he'd seen of Samson slaying a thousand men with the jawbone of an ass, but the wild-eyed manslayer he imagined took the face of Colonel Lane, not Sam Wood. Lane was a hard man to figure. *He had powerful friends— he betrayed them, Atchison and that bunch, or maybe they betrayed him. Still, how could a man with a sense of right and wrong...?* It was a question that didn't frame itself for easy pondering.

"How do you figure that Colonel Lane, preacher?"

"The Lord don't leave all his work to just the righteous folk, I don't reckon."

Butler knew right and wrong had nothing to do with it. Lane didn't have a conscience. He wasn't pro-slavery. He wasn't abolition. He had thrown in his lot with the side he figured to win, pure and simple.

I'd follow Colonel Lane to hell and back. And once I made it out of hell, I would come back to help Aunt

Delphie. He was caught by surprise that he'd come to admire her in this last day. She didn't have any of the things he wanted for himself, no fine clothes, no fancy house. Like Reuben, she didn't ask for much. She had a shack and a milk cow and a piece of dirt where she could scratch out a few vegetables and a chance to do the Lord's work by helping runaways. Even a week ago, Blanche could scarcely contain his contempt for uneducated and illiterate field hands, like Reuben and Aunt Delphie. How could a life like hers be anything but a well of sorrows?

The south wind had borne him over the sea of grass and spilled him out on this eastern shore—it was all so real—and he had brought with him some wrong-headed ideas about freedom. But it wasn't Wood, it wasn't Lane or the Reverend Butler that lifted the scales from his eyes—it was Aunt Delphie. He was glad that he and Butler were alone. He felt shame, as if he had just become aware that he was naked.

She was at peace, and she was freer than any black person he'd ever known. She did what she wanted to do. She helped runaways. *That's a woman with gumption. If Butler had half the gumption Aunt Delphie does, he'd be back in Westport, pulling sixteen-penny nails out of his church house door.*

Blanche squinted as he turned his face away from the river and could see Butler standing dark above him, outlined by the sun. He was calling to Blanche, pleading as if from the pulpit, "Won't yah come? Won't yah come?"

"Sam Wood and the colonel are never going to get those Bibles up the riverbank. Not without a couple more strong backs."

"What do you want to do?"

"I want to put a shackle around the neck of Thomason and Atchison. But first, I'm going to teach that old woman to read."

"You're free now, son. You don't owe nothing to nobody."

"Preacher, in a couple of weeks, she'll be reading Shakespeare."

Butler shook his head. "There's folks all over that can't read a lick."

"Our work's over there. Get back in the skiff, preacher."

Butler hesitated, but soon he loosened the rope from the snag and took his place in the bow of the boat once again. Blanche rowed, west this time, back across the muddy, swirling torrent, back into the teeth of the conflict, to the place where Aunt Delphie waited for him on the quay.

AUTHOR'S NOTE

Blanche Kelso Bruce

At the beginning of the Civil War, Blanche Kelso Bruce attempted to enlist in the Northern army but was turned away because he was African American. Some biographies say he had been freed, others say he ran away. He settled in Lawrence, Kansas, and organized the state's first school for African Americans. In 1874, Mississippi elected him to the US Senate. Bruce was the first African American senator to preside over a Senate session, and he became the first African American senator to serve a full term.

Bruce was appointed as Registrar of the Treasury and served from 1881–85. His signature appeared on the paper money that the government began issuing during the Civil War. Bruce declined an offer to serve as ambassador to Brazil, as that country still practiced slavery. His public service continued in many other capacities until his death in 1898.

In 1856, Sam Wood helped drive the last nail in the Whig Party coffin when he traveled to Pittsburgh to serve as a delegate to the first Republican National Convention. He attended the Philadelphia convention that chose Fremont as its candidate for president. Wood helped organize the Atchison, Topeka and Santa Fe Railway, served as a colonel for the Union in the Civil War, and was speaker of the Kansas House of Representatives. And after a lifetime of his advocacy, by 1887, women were allowed to vote in every municipal election in Kansas. In 1891, Wood was murdered at the Methodist Church in Hugoton, Kansas, where he and his wife had gone to answer a summons. Wood died in his wife's arms, first shot in the back and again in the face by a political adversary. His killer never stood trial.

As sheriff of Douglas County, Kansas, Samuel Jones besieged Lawrence in the fall of 1855. He and the border ruffians turned away when they realized that Colonel Jim Lane had supervised the construction of battlements and that the citizens of Lawrence were armed to the teeth with Sharp's rifles. In May of the following year, Jones gathered a posse of 750 pro-slavery forces, and this time he successfully entered Lawrence. After they destroyed two printing presses, he set his posse to the task of bringing down the magnificent Free State Hotel that had been used to house a makeshift group that called itself the Free State Legislature. The honor of firing the first shot was given to "Staggering Davy" Atchison, who fired from a cannon stationed on the east side of Massachusetts Street. It failed to hit the building. The hotel withstood more than fifty shots without damage. A falling piece of masonry claimed the life of a border ruffian, the sole fatality in the campaign. Thereafter, the hotel was looted and set afire under two flags, one blood red and inscribed "Southern Rights" and the other, the Stars and Stripes.

Jim Lane recruited the first black men to wear a federal uniform for the Civil War. His troops called him the Grim Chieftain. The first Kansas Colored Infantry was mustered into the US Army at Fort Scott, Kansas, and fought Missouri bushwhackers more than two months prior to the time Lincoln authorized the enlistment of African Americans. Lane, now a general, gained a reputation for ferocity. He was hated in Missouri. After the Civil War, he served as a Kansas US senator, but he lost favor in Kansas and surrendered his life to his own hand in 1866.

The Good Guys

None of the events in this story actually happened to Blanche Bruce. The young Blanche Bruce in this book is a composite. Aunt Delphie is a composite character also.

Sam Wood, the fighting Quaker, was a real person. So too was Colonel Jim Lane, who suffered from a textbook case of psychosis. He might not have been a good man, but Providence used him like a fiery sword. Hollywood portrayed Lane as a bloodthirsty tyrant in a Clint Eastwood movie, *The Outlaw Josey Wales*. Reverend Butler and the lawyer Phillips were actual people. *Three Links of Chain* fictionalizes the actions of these men but depicts their place in history authentically.

Reuben and Sally were real people who were killed in the manner described but not in Westport. A runaway's escape from a corrupt conductor and a bootless sheriff actually happened, but not in Nebraska City and not to Blanche Bruce.

The Bad Guys

Atchison, Jones, Stringfellow, and Thomason were real people, but Thomason's given names were not Horace Archlewis. Their actions were fictionalized in *Three Links of Chain*, but the story depicts their place in history faithfully.

Kaw Nation, Kanza Nation

A Siouan tribe, the People of the South Wind migrated to the plains in the early seventeenth century. The names Kanza and Kaw were both used. To this day, the Kansas River also goes by the name Kaw River. Lewis and Clark (1804) estimated the tribal population of the Kaw to be fifteen hundred persons. Their depiction in *Three Links of Chain* is not accurate. Ten years before, in 1846, the Kaw Nation sold their tribal lands. So by 1855, the Kaw had been removed to the vicinity of Council Grove, Kansas, too far west on the Santa Fe Trail for a runaway to encounter them.

Twenty-one Kaw tribesmen lost their lives in service to the Union in the Civil War.

In 1873, the tribe was again removed, this time to lands in Indian Territory. Only 533 men, women, and children completed the journey to what is now Kay County in north central Oklahoma. By 1888, their population had declined to 188. Charles Curtis, a politician with mixed-Kaw ancestry, served as vice president under Herbert Hoover. In 2015, the tribe had approximately 3,350 members.

Actual Events

The term *Bleeding Kansas* was coined by Horace Greeley of *The New York Times* to describe the violence in Kansas Territory from 1854 to 1858. Beecher's Bibles, the press thrown in the river at Parkville, Stringfellow's Expedition (the stolen election), the molestation of the pioneer women, the killing of the peppery redhead Dow—these were accurate depictions of actual events. Lane arrived in Kansas just days after the stolen election.

While most states began using a secret ballot after 1884, Kentucky held on to its oral ballot until 1891.

The origin of the term *Jayhawker* is shrouded in uncertainty. It had been used eighty years earlier to describe followers of a Revolutionary War patriot, John Jay. For the sake of accuracy, it should be noted that Jayhawker did not have widespread currency in Kansas until 1858, when the opponents of the bush-whackers began to band together as vigilantes. Not all the Jayhawkers' motives were pure. Some, like Wild Bill Hickok, wore knee-high red yarn leggings over their boots. They came to be known as Red Legs and had a well-deserved reputation for the viciousness of their reprisals.

Lawrence

During the Civil War, a steady stream of Missouri runaways traveled through Lawrence, the county seat of Douglas County, Kansas. Lawrence became the target of pro-slavery aggression on three occa-sions. During the War, Lawrence's Free State Hotel was burned to the ground for a second time by an irregular band of marauders. Their leader, William Quantrill, was intent on capturing Jim Lane and skinning him alive. They were considered irregular because Missouri did not withdraw from the Union. They'd ceased to be called border ruffians and now dubbed themselves "bushwhackers," or "Quantrill's Raiders."

The cold reality is that on that day, 160 inno-cents were slaughtered by Quantrill's Raiders. Some accounts place the death toll at two hundred.

In the aftermath, the bushwhackers boasted that

Jim Lane had escaped in his nightshirt, running through a cornfield like a coward. Perhaps after your gang kills 160 innocent people, you need to make someone look small to make yourself look tall.

Hollywood has struggled with its interpretation of the Lawrence Massacre in film. Republic Pictures depicted it in 1940 in a romance/western called *Dark Command*. It starred John Wayne and pitted him in a love triangle/rivalry with Will Cantrell (Walter Pidgeon). The supporting cast included Roy Rogers and Gabby Hayes. The critically acclaimed *Ride with the Devil* (1999) was directed by Ang Lee and starred Tobey Maguire as a bushwhacker. In this film, the hero helps sack Lawrence, finds love (played by Jewel), and changes his nature from bushwhacker to peace lover.

As far as Americans killing innocent Americans goes, few events in our short history compare with Quantrill's raid on Lawrence. In 1868, George Armstrong Custer led an assault on a band of Cheyennes that came to be known as the Black Kettle Massacre. The highest estimate of dead came from Custer himself: 150. Custer's luck ran out, you might recall, when he attempted to recreate his glory in Wyoming, on the banks of the Little Bighorn. Bad luck for Custer: by 1876, the Indians were armed.

Then in 1995, Timothy McVeigh engineered the Murrah Building bombing in Oklahoma City that killed 168.

Kansas and Race

To its everlasting shame, Kansas held onto ugly vestiges of racial division. In 1953, the US Supreme Court struck down school segregation. Topeka, the state's capitol, was the defendant in the leading case. Kansans accepted the decision, but southern states organized violent resistance. To keep the peace, the president deployed the 101st Airborne Division to Arkansas and federalized the Arkansas National Guard. That President was Dwight D. Eisenhower, Kansas' favorite son, whose parents met at Lane University. It is told that Jim Lane was given the namesake honor of the college for his promise of a substantial endowment, but that he shot himself before he could fulfill his pledge.

Kansas and Politics

Before the Civil War, slavery's support was found in the Democratic Party, which had earned loyalty for expanding suffrage to all white men, not just landowners. Their opposition was in the Whig Party, a short-lived coalition held together by little more than their opposition to the Democrats. The Republican Party was born in 1856 out of the ashes of the Whig Party, but it was joined by disaffected "free soil" Democrats who opposed the expansion of slavery.

Disdain for Democrats ran deep in Kansas for years. The state has been a Republican stronghold in national races since the Civil War. In the historic 2008 Presidential election, only three out of 105 Kansas counties voted for the Democratic candidate, Barack Obama. Douglas County went with the Democrats.

The mother of the man who became our first African American president, as well as her parents and her grandparents, all hailed from Kansas.